CLEAN SWEEP

The Inside Story of the ZZZZ Best Scam . . .
One of Wall Street's Biggest Frauds

The author's proceeds from sales of this book—except for court approved expenses—will be assigned to the victims of the ZZZZ Best scandal.

CLEAN SWEEP

The Inside Story of the ZZZZ Best Scam . . .
One of Wall Street's Biggest Frauds

Barry Minkow

THOMAS NELSON PUBLISHERS
Nashville • Atlanta • London • Vancouver

Published in Nashville, Tennessee, by Thomas Nelson, Inc., Publishers, and distributed in Canada by Word Communications, Ltd., Richmond, British Columbia, and in the United Kingdom by Word (UK), Ltd., Milton Keynes, England.

Unless otherwise noted, Scripture quotations are from the HOLY BIBLE, NEW INTERNATIONAL VERSION®. Copyright © 1973, 1978, 1984 by International Bible Society. Used by permission of Zondervan Bible Publishing House. All rights reserved.

The "NIV" and "New International Version" trademarks are registered in the United States Patent and Trademark Office by International Bible Society. Use of either trademark requires the permission of International Bible Society.

Scripture quotations noted TLB are from *The Living Bible* (Wheaton, Illinois: Tyndale House Publishers, 1971) and are used by permission.

Teddy Stallard story from *Who Switched the Price Tags?*, Dr. Anthony Campolo, 1986, Word, Inc., Dallas, Texas. All rights reserved.

Library of Congress Cataloging-in-Publication Data

Minkow, Barry.
  Clean sweep : the inside story of the ZZZZ best scam—one of Wall Street's
  biggest scams / Barry Minkow.
    p. cm.
  ISBN 0-7852-7916-4
  1. Minkow, Barry. 2. Businessmen—United States—Biography.
  3. Converts—United States—Biography. 4. Success in business—United
  States. 5. Fraud—United States. 6. Wall Street. I. Title.
  HC102.5.M5A3 1995
  364.1 '68—dc20   94–42957
                                                                 CIP

Printed in the United States of America

1 2 3 4 5 6 7 — 01 00 99 98 97 96 95

Disclaimer

This is not an exhaustive account of every detail of the ZZZZ Best case. It was not my intention to reenact every facet of my crime, but rather to focus on critical events that shaped and changed my life.

Upon the advice of my publisher and others, I have chosen to change the names of most individuals listed in CLEAN SWEEP, and I have also attempted to avoid calling specific attention to details concerning people, places, and events. Although the story told here is true, after so many years have passed and so many changes have occurred in my life and the lives of others, I do not wish to subject so many individuals to more publicity.

To refresh my memory of certain events, I used court documents, the ZZZZ Best Prospectus (with all its addenda), press clippings, and personal interviews with key people.

I spent almost three years on this project, hoping to give a fair and accurate presentation of my life story. However, I am not inerrant. With so many people involved, and with events occurring simultaneously, it is difficult to achieve perfection. Therefore, if I have misrepresented any incident, it was not my intention and I ask for forgiveness.

Dedication

For Peanut, who taught me more than he ever realized.
He was always willing to help and to inspire.
Maybe that's why the Lord needed him so soon.

And for Lili, who changed her dad's focus from the imperfect and temporary, which is scratched together here on earth, to the perfect and everlasting, which is freely given from Heaven.

Contents

Foreword

This is a book about compromise, corruption, collapse, and comeback. I began this project in 1991 while incarcerated at the Federal Correctional Institution in Englewood, Colorado. Two things motivated me to write: First, a few close friends who thought my autobiography might provide encouragement and hope to those who were hurting; and second, my observation, during my years in prison, that most inmates, though from very diverse backgrounds, share at least one thing in common—none of us ever *planned* on coming to prison.

Many are surprised to learn that our prisons today are filled with doctors, lawyers, bankers, accountants, and other professional people who began their careers with the best of intentions. Good schools, hard work, and long hours were their trademark, and success was the payoff. But something happened along the way. Many of them, like me, can pinpoint a time when they fell prey to the temptation to *compromise*. In some cases, it was a subtle departure from the legitimate, but a departure nonetheless.

As compromise continues, it inevitably leads to *corruption*. During this phase of the anatomy of failure, cheating, manipulating, and deceit become easier and easier. Finally, these activities are fully manifested in *collapse*. That's when it comes time to "pay the piper," which often involves the embarrassment and humiliation of prison. For many, that's where the story ends. They believe life is over and change is a fruitless task because, after all, no one believes those "I've-seen-the-light-in-prison" stories anyway.

But for those of us who cut our losses, made a change, and received Jesus Christ, this is not the case. Prison doesn't become the end—but the beginning of *comeback!* Surprisingly, the entrance requirements for a relationship with Jesus Christ are low. Although society is intolerant of those who have failed in the past,

He is not. Jesus will accept anyone who has a real desire to turn from sin and embrace *Him*. I make no apologies for falling into that category of people who have done just that. And this is my story . . .

Acknowledgments

There isn't room enough to thank all the people who encouraged and assisted me through this three-year writing process. To begin, I want to thank Skip and Carol Leifer, who, in 1991, first convinced me that I needed to sit down and write my life story—no matter how long it took. And then there's Bill and Jan Oudemolen, who visited me every week at FCI Englewood—when nobody else did. I want to thank Joe Mano, who pushed me to continue—when I felt like quitting. My mom and dad are also heroes in my life and are deserving of the highest praise. I love them both, and despite how badly I treated them during the ZZZZ Best days, they forgave.

Words can never express how much my editor, Dan Hatch, has meant to me. Rather than write the book for me, he took the time and taught me how to write. His patience, love, and professionalism made this project fun. I only hope that we can work together again. My agent, Clint Horsley, who patiently communicated with the publisher on my behalf while I was in prison, is deserving of much thanks. I'd also like to thank Randy Long, my lawyer, who worked hard to set up my victim-relief fund with the United State's Attorney's Office. And I cannot forget David Kenner, my criminal lawyer, who visited me every day while I was in the "hole" at Terminal Island. I'll always love you, David.

Finally, I'd like to thank Shaun Redgate, who has taken over Peanut's job as my best friend. Without Shaun, I would have never been able to complete my education or publish this book. May God bless him, his wife Melody, and their four children.

PART 1:
Compromise

Out of Control 1

I'll call him back," I yelled to Amy, my long-time secretary. The last person in the world I wanted to talk to before the biggest weekend of my life was Thomas Meyer.

It wasn't that I didn't respect Thomas, for his financial public-relations work for my company had rapidly propelled ZZZZ Best's stock from four dollars to over eighteen dollars a share. But I really didn't want another of his long lectures on how to handle the investment bankers during the upcoming three-day convention.

I glanced at my watch and saw that it was already 4:00 P.M. I had only thirty minutes to drive from the ZZZZ Best corporate headquarters to the softball field, where a girls' team I sponsored and coached would play for the league championship. I wanted to be sure to get there early enough to give them a pep talk.

After the game I would go immediately to the hotel to help with the final details and greet guests arriving for the convention.

Stopping at her desk, I gave Amy some last-minute instructions: "If Phil or Stan calls, send word to me at the softball game so I can get back to them immediately. If anyone else calls, tell them I'm at the hotel, preparing for the incoming guests."

Philip Cox and Stanley Robbins were the men behind the scenes who had "made" Barry Minkow. They had provided financing and direction to ZZZZ Best in the early years, and now they had "off-the-record" control of the company—and of me. Their alleged affiliation with East Coast criminal elements had instilled the necessary fear that assured them of my loyalty.

As I rushed out of the office, Amy called after me in a concerned, motherly tone, "Have you eaten yet?"

"Yes, dear!" I lied as I ran to my Ferrari, then squealed out of the parking lot.

❖ ❖ ❖

I cranked the car stereo way up and began to picture in my mind just how I planned to pull off the biggest con of my life. The loud music always helped clear my head.

The convention was going to cost over $850,000. The goal for the weekend was to convince a large investment banking firm that even though I was only twenty-one, I could successfully run the $300 million-plus public company that would emerge when ZZZZ Best completed acquisition of KeyServ, Inc. ZZZZ Best was half the size of KeyServ, Inc., and the average age of our management team was half of theirs. The combined companies would employ over 3,300 people, so the concerns of the investment firm and their management were well-founded. Before they raised over $40 million to finance this acquisition, they wanted the assurance of a smooth transition.

The convention would show them firsthand how well the complete management teams of both companies could work together. To accomplish this, I'd flown in all the top KeyServ executives from all over the United States, along with the ZZZZ Best managers who were scattered throughout Arizona, Nevada, and northern and southern California. I'd even invited the spouses of some of the people, which brought the total number of participants to about eight hundred. I began to sweat and my heart rate increased as I thought of the power and control that would soon be mine—if I performed well.

As I approached the softball field, I realized that before I could fully enjoy the weekend, I first had to win this championship softball game. My sister Sheri, who assisted me as the team manager, was already warming up the players, girls between the ages of thirteen and fifteen. When Sheri had asked me to sponsor the team, I had agreed under one condition—I had to run the show.

First, I spent thirty thousand dollars to restore their weed-infested field with new sod. Additionally, since few people showed up for these games, I routinely filled the stands by paying fifty dollars to each person who attended. It was a much greater challenge for me to coach a team with lots of people watching. The championship game would be no exception. When I drove up, I saw that the stands were flooded with fans.

The team we were to play was much better than we were, and everyone knew it. I also knew that their pitcher threw the ball so fast that our girls wouldn't even see it. To overcome this obstacle, my team needed a simple motivational speech. I had given the same talk to the employees at ZZZZ Best several times with great success, so it was bound to work this time too.

After warm-ups I gathered the team in the dugout and told them the Babe Ruth story: how one of the years he hit more home runs than anyone in the major leagues, he also struck out more than anyone. But because his home runs were more memorable than his strikeouts, the "Babe" was remembered as the great home-run hitter. In conclusion, I told the girls that by simply being in the championship game, they had already hit "the home run." By telling them that they were already winners, I hoped to take away the pressure they must be feeling.

As expected, the opposing pitcher all but shut us out through the first six innings. Although we were only down 3 to 1, our one run had come through a multitude of errors. Since the game would only last seven innings, I had to think of a way to make something happen—anything that would bring me victory. As the president, chief executive officer, and chairman of the board of a \$280-million public company, getting ready to close a \$40-million acquisition, surely I could figure out a way to win a softball game.

Before the bottom of the seventh inning (our last chance to catch up), I called one of my ZZZZ Best managers over to the dugout. He was in charge of paying the fans. I had come up with a plan for victory. I instructed him to get the fans to make so much noise that their thirteen-year-old pitcher would get frustrated and walk all of our batters.

"We can't do that, Barry. She's just a little girl," he protested.

I stared him in the eye and yelled, "You can and you will get those fans on their feet or you'll be in the unemployment line on Monday morning! Do you get that, pal?" I was serious and he knew it. He'd learned at the office that winning—no matter what the cost—was the only way I did business.

"Yes, sir," he said, and he proceeded to motivate the fans. They began to scream and stamp so loudly that the little thirteen-year-old became visibly shaken, despite her own coach's encouragement. I didn't feel sorry for her loss of composure because, as far as I was concerned, she was the enemy.

To apply more pressure to the pitcher, I sent my girls up to bat left-handed. This strategy worked as she walked the fourth batter, which scored a run. Now we were behind just 3 to 2. My next batter struck out, and the crowd quieted down a bit. I stormed out of the dugout, waving at the crowd and demanding loud cheering. And that's what I got. The next batter, the best hitter on the team, was allowed to bat right-handed, but I told her to take a strike.

She didn't listen, swung, and hit a soft ground ball between first and second base. It would have been a routine play if my fans hadn't been yelling at the tops of their lungs and intimidating the players. After three throwing errors, two more runs scored and the game was over. We'd won! It hadn't been pretty, but when it came to winning, for me the ends definitely justified the means.

Throughout the game I hadn't once thought about all my problems. I had temporarily forgotten my involvement with the underworld and the lies and deceit that had helped build ZZZZ Best.

After a brief celebration with the players, I left for the hotel. *One victory down and one to go,* I thought. As I drove, I noticed that my throat was extremely sore. I tried to clear it but to no avail. I had yelled so much during the softball game that I was practically voiceless. I wasn't worried though. The fate of my company was in my hands, and nothing was going to stop me from getting the forty million dollars—certainly not a sore throat.

I arrived at the hotel shortly after 7:00 P.M. Several of my employees were setting up the room for the big convention, and people descended on me from every angle, asking for advice and direction regarding tasks that needed to be completed before the big kickoff, twelve hours away.

The stage was neatly set with a map of the United States in the background. Small colored lightbulbs marked each state that would have ZZZZ Best/KeyServ carpet-cleaning outlets upon the closing of the merger. To the left and right of the map were large television screens, strategically placed so that all eight hundred people could see me perform. Three of our new company vans—with their ZZZZ Best logos—were displayed along with our equipment, around the auditorium.

I built this company from nothing, I bragged to myself. And now I was about to reap the benefits of my labors. My "stage" had finally been set.

After greeting a few guests, I rushed up to my room to watch my most recent anti-drug commercial, filmed earlier in the week. I never liked to miss my television appearances. Then I returned to give my management team some last-minute instructions, and finally went to bed. It had been a long day, and the convention was to start with a 7:00 A.M. breakfast. I needed to be ready, and I would be, sore throat or no sore throat.

Falling asleep was difficult. For two months I had looked forward to May 7, 8, and 9 of 1987, and my anxiety made rest impossible. When morning finally came, I walked down to breakfast, tired but on time. People from across the country sat at their tables, anxiously wondering what awaited them over the next few days. As the meal ended, they found their assigned seats in the auditorium. It was, as we L.A. Laker fans say (or used to say), *show time!*

The convention kicked off with a dramatic introduction—of me. My longtime sales trainer described with enthusiasm all the "titles" I had earned through the years. Then the lights dimmed, and the two big-screen TVs showed video clips from the many television programs on which I had appeared, followed by our television commercials, run one after the other.

I discreetly surveyed the room. The corporate finance people seemed to be enjoying the introduction. In the back, tucked away behind one of the vans, was my bodyguard—Phil Cox—scanning the crowd. The KeyServ people were smiling and applauding the commercials. It was working.

Knowing exactly when the video would end, I rose from my seat and walked slowly toward the stage. I remembered the days in the garage and the times when the payroll checks had bounced. I thought back to when I had met Donald Snyder and received the first of many high-interest loans. I recalled the nice lady at Western Hills Savings and Loan whom I had lied to in order to secure a six-plus-million-dollar loan. I even remembered the expression on the face of the defeated pitcher in the recent softball game. And if I had had it to do all over again at that point—as I climbed onto the stage—I wouldn't have changed a thing.

The crowd came to their feet, applauding wildly. The ZZZZ Best managers began chanting, "Barry . . . Barry . . . Barry!" This was the moment I had dreamed of all my life. Here I was,

the youngest ever to start a public company, at the age of nineteen, and the current "Wonder Boy" of Wall Street, finally getting the recognition I thought I deserved. When the audience
quieted down, I began bragging about the accomplishments of
ZZZZ Best. I boldly proclaimed that upon the completion of the
KeyServ/ZZZZ Best merger, the new company would be the
largest nonfranchised carpet-and-furniture-cleaning company in
the United States.

At that moment the map lights flashed on, and the whole
crowd once again sprang to their feet. I then introduced the two
corporate-finance people and stated that only they stood in the
way of making the ZZZZ Best dream become a reality. I was
right where I wanted to be. If the deal was going to get done,
my speech and each of the next three days had to go perfectly. But
since speaking and motivating large audiences were my strongest
talents, I had everything under control. I was about to close the
biggest deal of my young life.

Despite my sore throat, the words flowed smoothly. After
emphasizing how rapidly our company had grown over the past
five years, I continued by focusing on our future goals. "We're
going to the top, people," I said enthusiastically, "and you're on
the ground floor. Tell me . . . do you want to be 'ZZZZ Best'?"
The crowd once again jumped to their feet, cheering hysterically
and chanting, "ZZZZ Best . . . ZZZZ Best . . . ZZZZ Best."

When I concluded my speech, ZZZZ Best employees approached the investment people and proclaimed their love and
admiration for me and the company. And the momentum built
from there. All the scheduled events went off flawlessly, and three
days later, the once-skeptical investment bankers left the hotel,
confident that the ZZZZ Best acquisition would be a success.

But I left the convention with far less optimism. Instead of
celebrating the culmination of my greatest con, feelings of loneliness overwhelmed me. As soon as I got home, I went upstairs to
the bedroom and lay down. I tried to recall the events of the past

three days: the dozens of standing ovations, the chanting of my name, the hundreds of happy people, and the promise of running the largest carpet-cleaning company in the nation. But all this, at least for now, had ended. The crowds were gone, the chanting had faded, and the peace and quiet of my spacious home closed in on me.

My mind began to wander. I wondered how many friends I would really have if people knew the truth about ZZZZ Best. No matter how hard I tried to suppress my feelings of shame and guilt, I couldn't. My conscience always waited for the action to stop before it kicked into gear.

I sat up, reached into the drawer of the nightstand, and pulled out several fan letters. In times like this, I found comfort in these complimentary letters. I scanned through three or four of them before stuffing them back into hiding. *If they only knew,* I thought. *If they only knew.*

I soon realized that being alone was making things worse. I needed to escape from guilt by surrounding myself with people who liked me and comforted me. I got up, went into the bathroom, and pulled out my secret stash of anabolic steroids. After ingesting nearly one hundred milligrams, I was ready for the gym. Though the pressure of running a public company kept me from a consistent workout program, steroids helped me retain both my size and strength.

I had heard about the potential side effects of steroid abuse, but I figured those horror stories were only to scare people away from them. I didn't care much about possible future problems. I was living for instant gratification, and the steroids filled that prescription perfectly. But the physical signs were there—if I chose to heed them. Within an eighteen-month period, I had been hospitalized three times for pneumonia and high fever. My immune system was severely damaged, and my kidneys ached on a daily basis. But because people noticed my power and physique, I ignored these side effects.

I climbed into my Testarossa and headed for the gym. The place was packed, and many of the guys greeted me warmly as I marched directly to the bench press and began warming up. The price of acceptance here was a strong bench press or a heavy squat. The irony was that each of us knew that the other attained his strength artificially—through steroids—but none of us ever admitted it.

Even though the past three days had drained me physically and emotionally, the steroids helped me overcome the fatigue, and I was able to do four reps at 335 pounds.

"Barry, you gonna max out today?" a friend asked.

"I'm pretty tired," I responded, "but I'm going for 375."

"I'll spot you when you're ready."

The more I got into my workout, the less I thought about the real Barry Minkow. Before I knew it, several guys had gathered to watch the big lift. To make it look good, I chalked my hands thoroughly, took some deep breaths, and even added to the on-lookers' cheers with a few yells as I slowly pushed the bar up from my chest. Once I had racked the weight, I enthusiastically sprang from the bench, tapped a few "high fives," and watched my audience return to their workouts. For a brief moment, it was like being on stage all over again.

Moving on to a different exercise, I noticed a man loading up the bench press on the other side of the gym—with 420 pounds! Guys came from everywhere to watch this young body-builder attempt this lift. I also watched, and was angry. Not only was this guy stronger than I, but he commanded a bigger audi-ence for his lift than I had for mine. And his form was so good as he smoothly pushed the weight up from his chest that you couldn't even tell if he was straining. I was the only one who didn't congratulate him as he got up from the bench. This guy had stolen my glory. I burned with envy and jealousy. I wasn't "zzzz best" weight lifter.

Nonetheless, I smiled, pretending that my recent defeat

hadn't hurt my pride. I was a master at putting on a front. I left the gym with the same external pride and confidence that had taken a one-man carpet-cleaning company in my parents' garage and built it into a success. Deep down inside, though, I knew the truth. ZZZZ Best was no more real than the 375-pound bench press I had just completed. Both my business and my body were lies built to mask my true self. I wasn't the invincible entrepreneur who had "the world by the tail," as so many thought. I was a scared, insecure twenty-one-year-old who did whatever it took to gain approval.

On the drive home, I realized that I was rapidly running out of confidence-building options. Neither reading my fan mail nor bench-pressing 375 pounds had comforted my damaged ego. But then I thought of Susan, Brenda, and Donna, the women in my life who gave me love and acceptance—two things I needed desperately. As far as I was concerned, having several girlfriends went hand in glove with big bucks.

I picked up my car phone and called Susan, a very pretty woman who had a unique way of making me feel good about myself, even when things were going badly. "Hi, sweetheart. This is Barry. How about dinner tonight?" I asked. We talked for a few minutes and after hearing the things I needed to hear— "I love you and want to see you"—I told her I'd be by at 6:00 P.M. to pick her up.

Next on my list was Brenda. Although she said we didn't have a lot in common, just being with her made my ego soar. Brenda's looks could light up a room. Whenever we went out, I really played up the "rich boy" image—just to impress her. "Hi, honey. Do you want to see me tonight?" I asked confidently over the car phone. Hearing her say yes allowed me to put more distance between my failure at the gym and my success with women. I agreed to pick her up at 8:30. After hanging up I thought back to my high school days.

I (and all of my friends) had wanted to date Brenda, but she wasn't interested in "high school boys." That all changed a few years later when I accidentally ran into her at a gift shop where she worked. Brenda had read about me in the newspaper, heard about my new five-thousand-square-foot house (with a *Z* tiled onto the bottom of the swimming pool), and was visibly impressed by the Ferrari I was driving.

No longer was I Barry Minkow, the high school "boy." The fame of ZZZZ Best had given me such wealth and power that even Brenda wanted to go out with me. This somehow seemed to make all the lying, cheating, and manipulating that went into building ZZZZ Best worthwhile.

Finally, I called home to speak with Donna, the woman I had lived with for the last two years, and the one I cared for the most. I glanced at my watch as the phone rang. It was 5:00 P.M. She was probably home from the convention by now.

"Hello?" she answered.

"Hi, Donna. Was I great, or what?" I asked arrogantly. Having witnessed my performance at the convention, she knew exactly what I was talking about.

"Of course you were, Barry." Her response was no surprise. She always supported me and only wanted to make me happy. Unfortunately, she had no idea just how difficult that task was. Donna never knew the truth about my dishonest and deceitful business tactics. Until, of course, it was too late.

Within minutes I was home, and my weight-lifting defeat was but a forgotten memory. Three women wanted to see me— all in the same night. I felt needed, loved, and accepted. The guilt and insecurity had been neutralized, at least for a little while. I greeted Donna with a quick kiss and ran upstairs to shower. Then I put on my usual Saturday night outfit—a tight tank top and shorts. My ego needed the constant bolstering of comments like "You look great, Barry" or "What a great body you have." I told Donna the usual lie about having a business meeting at some associate's house, but added that I'd be home before midnight to spend the night with her.

By breaking every known traffic law, I arrived at Susan's house at 6:00 P.M., with two thousand dollars cash in my pocket and a shining Ferrari. As Susan and I drove down Ventura Boulevard, everyone seemed to be watching us. Some recognized the familiar "ZZZZBST" license plates, and others remembered me from the commercials and television shows on which I had appeared. Heads turned left and right. *If there is a heaven, it can't be any better than this,* I thought.

Pulling up to a stoplight, I looked to my left and noticed an old, beat-up Toyota Tercel. The driver surveyed my bright red Ferrari and gave me a thumbs-up. I turned to Susan, looking beautiful beside me, then back to the guy in the Toyota. He seemed happy and at peace with himself. *What a fool,* I thought to myself. *How can anyone be content driving a dumpy, broken-down car like that? He probably works for the government in some forty-hour-a-week job and has no desire to be rich and famous.* He was infected with the disease of mediocrity and that, as far as I was concerned, was worse than death.

I loved having to rush through dinner with Susan so I could get to Brenda's house by 8:30. I felt so "in demand." We ate at a little French restaurant near her condo that I enjoyed primarily because they recognized me. After dinner I sped Susan back to her house, offering my standard excuse for cutting the night short: "Business calls, honey." But before I left, I promised her that even though I was living with Donna, she was the one I really loved. I didn't tell most of my girlfriends about my arrangement with Donna, but Susan knew better. I gave her a brief kiss good night and was off for Brenda's house.

It was 8:05, and I was right on time. As usual, I cranked my stereo and began to imagine how famous I would become, once the KeyServ acquisition was complete. Maybe Johnny Carson would finally let me on his show. Even though I had made the

Oprah Winfrey Show, the *Wall Street Journal,* and *Newsweek* magazine, my publicist couldn't seem to get me on Carson. But with this major acquisition, they had to invite me. And then I could move on to my next goal—owning a professional sports team. Although I ultimately wanted to purchase the Pittsburgh Steelers (my all-time favorite team), I knew I had to start smaller—and at the time that meant the Seattle Mariners.

By the time I snapped out of my dream world, I was in Brenda's driveway. I knocked on her door and when she opened it, I just stood there speechless. She looked great, and nothing was going to make me look better than to be seen with such a beautiful girl. I drove her to a Malibu beachfront restaurant in which I was supposedly a partner. At least that's what my behind-the-scenes partners told me.

Throughout the meal we talked about ZZZZ Best and my future goals. I don't think I ever once asked Brenda how she was or what she enjoyed doing. I was too wrapped up in myself to care about anyone else. As we drove home, Brenda insisted that we stop by my house so she could see it. I had been promising to show it to her for weeks, and now she was calling my bluff. So I wouldn't appear to be hiding anything (at the time, she didn't know about Donna), I agreed to a short visit.

My hands began to sweat as I thought about the possibility of Donna being home. It was 10:45 as I pulled up to the security gate at Westchester County Estates. By now Donna was sure to be out somewhere with her friends. The guard gave me his usual wave of recognition, and I proceeded toward my house. The first thing I noticed was that Donna's Mercedes was nowhere to be seen.

I took Brenda into the house and showed her the downstairs layout. Then she wanted to see the bedroom. I agreed, but explained that I needed a few minutes to straighten things up a bit. I quickly ran up to my room and, half panic-stricken, shoved Donna's clothes into the closet and her pictures into the drawer of the nightstand. I calmly strolled back down the stairs and brought Brenda up.

She admired the fireplace and the Jacuzzi and even sat on my king-sized waterbed. *If only the guys from Cleveland High could see me now,* I thought to myself. She wanted to stay longer but because I feared Donna's return, I hustled her out the door.

Within minutes we were on our way back to her house. On her doorstep I kissed her good-bye and promised that the following weekend we would spend more time together.

I was home by 11:45, fifteen minutes before my self-imposed deadline. Before I went to bed, I returned Donna's pictures and clothes to their original places. Shortly thereafter, when Donna came home, I immediately let her know how much I had missed her.

When she was in the bathroom getting ready for bed, I lay there and thought about the events that had transpired that evening. I had gone through so much just to bring some temporary happiness to my life, and now that it had ended, I was defenseless against the sudden feelings of disappointment and discouragement. I nervously tossed and turned, trying to pinpoint the missing piece in my life. Why couldn't I find contentment and peace when I had attained so much and far exceeded everyone's expectations? One thing was certain though: I was out of control, going ninety-five miles an hour in the fast lane of life, headed straight for disaster . . . and deep down I knew it.

Faking the Sale | 2

H i, my name is Barry, and I'd like to give you a free copy of the *Los Angeles Times Historical Headlines*."

I could barely see who I was talking to. *Another one of those houses with metallic screens that are impossible to see through,* I thought. The prospect cracked the door wide enough for me to slip her a complimentary copy of the newspaper. This was a good sign.

I knew instinctively to continue my pitch at this, the maximum point of curiosity. "The *Los Angeles Times* has agreed to sponsor a special educational trip to Yosemite National Park for the kids who get the most new subscriptions to their newspaper," I went on enthusiastically. "They've even lowered their rates to make it easier for us to sign up new people."

Actually, I didn't care about some stupid trip to Yosemite—I was more interested in the one-dollar commission I would earn for each new subscription. At age nine, a dollar went a long way.

"Well, son," the lady said, "I'd love to help you get that trip, but I just cancelled my subscription to the *Times* because every morning I would find my paper out on the curb or under my car. I just got tired of the hassle."

An objection. I had to respond. Even though the boss had prohibited us from promising front-door delivery, I needed this sale, and this lady needed to hear how badly the *Times* wanted her business. I was determined not to take no for an answer—even if it meant lying.

"Okay, ma'am, since you're a dissatisfied customer—or *ex-*customer—I'm allowed to promise you front-door delivery *if you sign up during this special offer.* In fact, if your paper isn't delivered to your doorstep every day for the next six weeks, you don't have to pay anything," I declared boldly. I didn't care if she paid or not. I got my dollar when she signed up on my sheet.

"Are you sure about this money-back guarantee?" she asked as she stepped out onto the porch.

"Yes, ma'am," I lied, as I looked at her with all my nine-year-old innocence. "And if you sign up, you'll be helping me earn the trip to Yosemite." The minute she smiled, I knew the sale was mine. I could step off the gas pedal now and just let her do the rest.

"What's your name?" she asked.

"My name is Barry. Barry Minkow."

"And where do you live, Mr. Barry Minkow?" Her voice was friendly, and she seemed genuinely interested in me.

"I live in Reseda on Lull Street. My boss drove me and a few other kids over to your neighborhood."

"Well, Mr. Minkow, you can tell your boss that I said you did a great job of selling me." She grabbed my clipboard, filled out the sign-up sheet, and handed it back to me. "When you get older, you're going to make a heck of a salesman." She patted me on the shoulder and I was on my way.

As I walked to the next house, one of my fellow employees called my name from across the street. "Hey, Barry, how many sales have you made today?" he asked in a competitive tone.

"I just got my third one," I bragged.

"That's all? I've already got five! I knew I was a better salesman than you. That top-salesman award you won last month was pure luck. I'm going to win this month!" he said as he walked up the next driveway.

Darn! I said to myself. *How could he make five sales in less than three blocks?* If I was going to stay on top, I needed at least three more sales before we checked in with the boss.

Aggressively setting off down the block, walking from house to house faster and with greater determination, I longed for the opportunity to sell. And I did. In fact, I hit two in a row, but that only tied me with "the enemy." I needed to win!

Finally, I came to the end of the block and my last chance at victory. I rang the doorbell. No one answered. *Maybe it's broken,* I thought. So I opened the screen and slammed my knuckles against the wooden door. No one was home and I knew it, but I couldn't accept that. I looked down at my clipboard and the blank space where my sixth sale should have gone glared at me from the page.

Just as I was preparing myself for defeat, something occurred to me. What if I were to use the address of this last house, make up some name, and write it up just like the other leads? No one would probably ever know, and even if my boss did find out, I'd say it was the customer's fault for writing down the wrong address. At nine years of age, I couldn't possibly keep track of every house! Besides, anything was better than facing failure.

I sat down on the porch, looked around to make sure no one was watching, and began to fill in my sixth sale of the day, using my previous leads as models for what a legitimate sale should look like. I even forged a fake signature. As soon as I was done— it took me all of five minutes—I walked quietly to the corner where I was to be picked up by my boss.

My competitor was already there, smiling broadly. "Did you get any more?" I asked cautiously.

"No, but I didn't need to. I've still got you beat," he said confidently as the minitruck pulled up to the curb to take us home.

I took great pleasure in holding up my clipboard. "I don't think so, my friend. Maybe next time."

His face lost all color as we jumped into the back of the truck.

As we pulled away, I was amazed at how easy it was for me to separate in my mind *how I had won* from *the fact that I had won.*

❖   ❖   ❖

"It's for you, Barry," Mom said as I ran to the kitchen and picked up the phone.

"Who is it?" I asked curiously.

"I think it's your boss from the *L.A. Times.*"

I took the phone and sat down at the nearby table. "Hello?"

"Hi, Barry. I wanted to talk to you about one of the sales you made last week," he said in a calm voice. "Do you have a minute?"

A feeling of nausea quickly overwhelmed me. He had found out about the phony lead. "Yes, sir, I—I've got a minute," I stuttered, forcing the words through my fear.

"First of all, I want to tell you what a great job you're doing for me. You're the best salesman out there."

"Thank you." His encouragement helped me relax.

"But I had a problem in trying to confirm one of your leads. It seems as though the lady you put down—I think her name is Malone—doesn't live at the address you specified. Now, Barry, you didn't make this sale up, did you?"

"Of course not," I said defensively. "Is that what you think I did?"

"Look, Barry, it's pretty obvious that the lead is a phony, and I can't afford to pay you a commission on a fake sale." He paused. "Do you need a little extra money or something?"

How wrong he was. I hadn't created the sale to make a dollar. I had done it so I could be the best! But as I sat there at the kitchen table I was embarrassed. The other kids would surely find out about what I had done. How could I face them? *I just can't go back to work,* I thought.

"No, I don't need any extra money," I denied. "In fact, my

mom and dad don't even like me working at such a young age. Just keep the money you owe me, and we'll call it even."

"Hey, Barry, I don't want you to quit. I just want you to be honest. You've got a lot of talent and can go a long way when you grow up—but not if you take shortcuts," he said compassionately.

Shortcuts . . . there was that word again. Dad used it often to describe the way I did my household chores. Instead of emptying all the trash cans, I'd just do the ones I knew he'd see. One of my teachers at Cantara Street Elementary School had also used the term *shortcut* to describe the inconsistency in my homework assignments. An old basketball coach explained that although I had the talent to be a starting varsity player, the shortcuts I took during practices kept me on the *junior* varsity squad. In addition, the teacher for my upcoming bar mitzvah often complained that I constantly resorted to various shortcuts in my studies. Yes, this nine-year-old had become quite familiar with the term.

"I understand what you're saying, but summer vacation is almost over and I need to do a few things before school starts," I lied. "Maybe next year I can work for you."

The disappointment in his response was obvious. "Maybe, Barry, but I want you to know that I'm your friend, not your enemy. I'll send you a check in the mail for last week's work. Take care of yourself."

After I hung up, I went to my room. As I lay there on the bed, staring at the Pittsburgh Steelers pennant hanging across my closed door, I thought about my decision to quit. Why was I always the one who went through such difficult times? Most of my friends lived normal, happy, uneventful lives, and yet mine seemed plagued by controversy and instability. For some reason I was never satisfied with following everyone else's lead.

Maybe that's why my pediatrician had me on Ritalin—to defuse those urges when they got out of control, especially in the classroom. As I thought back over the events of the past several days, I focused on the words of the nice lady who had complimented me on my salesmanship: "When you get older, you're going to make a heck of a salesman."

I wondered what she meant, and how she knew.

❖   ❖   ❖

Forty-five, fifty-five, sixty miles per hour . . . *wow!* I never thought Dad's little Fiat convertible could go that fast, especially with four people stuffed into it. Then again, I never thought I'd be going to an exclusive, private military school with a bunch of rich kids during my early junior high school years. To subsidize this expensive education, my father had joined a car pool that required him to take two other students to and from school each day. And that meant the cozy storage space behind the seats for me—uniform and all. Our family pediatrician had suggested military school as the only remaining option. After years of private counseling, child-guidance clinics, and even Ritalin had failed to control my behavior, the last hope for hyperkinetic Barry Minkow was a strict military school.

The promises made to my parents by the staff at the military school were threefold: I would learn discipline, self-control, and leadership. My problem up until seventh grade was lack of self-control. The classroom was like a stage for me; I answered questions out of turn and cracked jokes constantly. Nothing made me feel better than to make people laugh and then bask in their attention. As long as my classmates knew who Barry Minkow was, I was satisfied. Unfortunately, the principal also knew who Barry Minkow was—I was a regular visitor to his office during my first six years of school. Teachers seemed to lose patience with me, too, as I competed for attention. It wasn't a learning disability—my grades were fine—but a desire for attention that required my constantly seeking approval from my peers.

Of all my childhood experiences, military school impacted my life the most. Until that time I hadn't been exposed to great wealth, nor was I aware of the effects money had on people. Many successful businessmen in our area sent their sons and daughters to the military school. In fact, the majority of the students came from the wealthy areas of Encino, Woodland Hills, and Tarzana. In contrast, I lived in Reseda, a modest Valley suburb where the average income was significantly less than the towns south of Ventura Boulevard.

Adjustment was very difficult for me at the military school. The kids constantly questioned why my dad drove a cheap Fiat and my mom a Dodge Dart. They made it seem as if there were something wrong with not having a Cadillac or Mercedes. My reaction was to do what I thought every young teenager would do in seeking the acceptance of his classmates—I lied! Being poor was just not cool in the eyes of the wealthy girls. I found myself deeply concerned with what other people thought of me and made up story after story about how rich my father was. However, the reality was quite the opposite. It was the 1979–80 school year, interest rates were in double digits, and my dad was quickly put out of the real estate business. In fact, things were so bad he had to borrow from my grandmother to keep me in the school.

Consequently, I harbored a great deal of resentment toward my father throughout my military school days. Why wasn't he like all my friends' fathers who drove Cadillacs and owned beautiful homes? Why was my father the "odd man out" when it came to material possessions? At the impressionable age of thirteen, I could only conclude that he simply wasn't as good as the other fathers. That's why I felt I had to lie and make him seem so much better.

By the end of my first year in military school, I was lying almost daily. I constantly made up stories, trying to get the attention of my female classmates. Seeing my friends leaving for home in their Rolls Royces and Mercedes Benzes prompted me to tell my father to pick me up at a parking lot across from the school, so no one would see his car. I told him he could avoid the traffic at school that way. But none of my ploys seemed to change things.

I began to entertain the thought that if my father couldn't make money, maybe I could. My mom worked for a carpet-cleaning company at that time, and she told me her boss might let me work there as a telephone solicitor during the summer. As my eighth-grade year came to a close, I knew some serious changes had to occur in the life of Barry Minkow.

Meanwhile, worsening financial problems at home brought my private school days to a close. It had taken me two years to make the transition from a public elementary school to a private academy. Now it was time for me to adjust back again. This time, though, I was scared. In addition to making new friends and getting accepted all over again, a different set of challenges awaited me at Northridge Junior High. Military school had protected me from the fights and drugs that were so prevalent in the public schools. At the junior high, money would not be the standard of acceptance, but traits like toughness and courage, both of which I lacked. So I decided to do something about my puny, 120-pound body. Heavily influenced by the then-popular *Incredible Hulk* television series, I determined that a regimented workout routine would bring me the physical confidence I so desperately needed.

However, to build up my body, I had to finance a health-club membership. Mom's job offer as a solicitor at the carpet-cleaning company began to look pretty good to me. Besides, I had something to prove to all those "rich kids" I had left behind at military school. While they would spend their summer vacations living off of mommy and daddy's funds, I would be earning my own money. Two years of making excuses for being poor had left me with a bitter resentment that could only be satisfied by out-performing those I had left behind. One day these guys were going to know who Barry Minkow was!

At age fourteen I started my job at Carpets Clean and began working out at a local health club. Thus, I was put in touch with both the people and the profession that would change my life forever.

A Different Ploy | 3

Carpets Clean occupied the second floor of an old, rundown office building. I worked the early shift, from 9:00 A.M. to 4:00 P.M., sitting at a table in a small, partitioned corner of the office with a push-button phone, three phone books, and several cross-street directories.

On the wall next to my desk hung a large chalkboard with all the names of the telephone solicitors. Next to each name was a grid columned off with the days of the week, upon which the solicitors kept track of their sales. This made it easier for the boss to monitor daily productivity. To me, though, it was simply a vehicle to let the whole office know that I was the *best* solicitor.

It didn't take me long to get the hang of it. Selling seemed to be in my blood. The more calls I made, the better I got at persuading people to have their carpets cleaned. My ego grew at a pace even with my salesmanship. When I topped the staff in leads for a given day, I made sure that everyone, including my mother, knew it. My confidence increased so rapidly that every time I made a call, I expected to make a sale.

Although my boss appreciated this arrogant attitude, the others in the office (with the exception of my mother) despised me. What was nothing more than a game to me was their livelihood. But I didn't care—as long as *I* could be the best!

After about eight weeks, my luck ran out. Instead of five or six sales a day, I dropped to only two or three. Other solicitors surpassed me, and my boss began to question my productivity. Faced with a damaged ego and the embarrassment of no longer being the best, I decided to take another shortcut.

All the sales and leads the solicitors obtained were to be written on four-by-six cards and filed in a sales box with separate compartments for each day of the month. We were also to post the leads in a book used to call back and resolicit past customers.

To circumvent this system and reestablish myself as the number-one solicitor, I created phony sales. That is, I actually sat at my table and, while talking to a dial tone, pretended to make sales. After slamming the receiver down in triumph, I would spring up from my chair and proclaim, "I got another one!" My coworkers believed my lies, just as others had when I had sold newspapers door-to-door for the *L.A. Times,* and when I had boasted to my military school friends about my father's wealth.

But it didn't take long for my fraud to be uncovered. After sending out several carpet-cleaning crews to homes where the residents denied making appointments, company management accused me of setting up phony sales. I vehemently denied any wrongdoing, affirming the authenticity of the leads. Because half of my leads were real and because of my age, the owner of the company didn't push the issue and even invited me back for the following summer. I had escaped another close call.

❖ ❖ ❖

With my public school debut only days away, I increased the intensity of my workouts at the gym. But gains in strength and size came slowly. After almost four months of rigorous training, I had gained only eight pounds—not nearly enough to defend myself from the tougher kids attending Northridge Junior High.

As a result, feelings of fear and intimidation overwhelmed me. The thought of losing a fight in front of my fellow classmates scared me more than anything else. I spent many sleepless nights thinking about how I would protect myself in this potentially violent environment.

To increase my courage, I went to movies like *Rocky* and *The Big Brawl,* where the underdog overcame and defeated the larger opponent. And I resolved to overcome my fear. Although not blessed with great muscle size, I did have the ability to manipulate people. Before school began, I decided to befriend guys who had spent their seventh- and eighth-grade years at Northridge Junior High, and who were well respected at the school.

I found a friend who fit this profile. He was smaller than I but a lot tougher, and he had several older brothers who watched out for him. He was a great friend who provided me with the confidence and the protection I craved. But I was using him, and that was wrong.

Surprisingly, ninth grade went very smoothly. With my sense of humor, I earned the "class clown" award and made friends easily. Unfortunately, money problems at home replaced my problem of fear. Our electricity, gas, and phone were shut off because we couldn't pay the bills. Dad couldn't find a job, making the tension at home nearly unbearable. My parents— Mom, concerned for our welfare; Dad, defending himself—argued constantly. My sisters, Sheri and Gail, used humor to get through these tough situations. Together we would laugh at my dad's financial problems and even make jokes about his unemployment. But I was crying on the inside. The last person I ever wanted to be was my father. Just five years earlier, no one would have questioned his authority. But as the money dwindled away, so did our respect for him. His leadership and credibility were undermined by his inability to provide for the family. As I watched this process unfold, I made mental notes. This was never going to happen to me.

As I now look back on this time in my life, I realize how bad my dad must have felt. But instead of providing encouragement,

I ridiculed him and thus became part of the problem, not part of the solution.

One occasion in particular sticks in my mind. Our gas had been turned off for lack of payment, and that meant no hot water for showers. My dad got the family together and asked us kids to spend the night at friends' houses, so we wouldn't be forced to take cold showers and live without heat. I recall thinking that I could react to this situation in one of two ways: with support and understanding or with disrespect and resentment. I chose the latter. I made it very clear to my dad that I would be extremely embarrassed to ask a fellow ninth-grade classmate to spend a school night at his house.

Up until then, the money problems hadn't actually separated me from my family. But now, the household would be forced to break up temporarily, to find different places to sleep. This had a profound effect on me as I felt a tug of loneliness pulling at my heart.

I called an old friend whom I had known for years, whose mother worked at a restaurant near my house. He was surprisingly understanding and invited me over for the night. As I said good-bye to my mom, she mentioned that she would be praying for me. *Praying for me?* I thought.

In my fourteen-year-old mind, there was a clear contradiction between the value of prayer and what I was going through. If there was a God, why did He allow these terrible things to happen to our family? That night, as I slept in an unfamiliar bed, I thought about this more and more. I concluded that if God existed, He certainly didn't care about Barry Minkow. Money, not God, was the solution to the family's and my problems. If we had the money we needed, then all the fighting, arguing, and separation would end. After vowing one more time that my children would never go through this, I fell asleep, with a rekindled determination to earn as much money as possible.

❖   ❖   ❖

While the rest of the kids in my class looked forward to a relaxing summer before starting high school, I looked forward to another summer at Mom's carpet-cleaning company—earning my own money.

That summer, in addition to telephone soliciting, I went out on jobs with the company's carpet cleaners. This was sales training for me, as I witnessed firsthand how to lie directly to someone's face and not think twice about it. We regularly told customers that their carpets were especially dirty and required extra treatment to get them clean, which would, of course, cost them extra money. Then we immediately hit the victims up for a "carpet protector." When applied properly, this product prevented rapid resoiling and increased the interval between cleanings. But since we were often out of carpet protector, we frequently sprayed water on the carpets and charged the customers for the real thing. I continued this practice through my first two years at ZZZZ Best.

That summer's weight lifting, on the other hand, was much more difficult for me. Although by now my strength had increased tremendously, I wasn't satisfied with how I looked. I had a big problem gaining weight and muscle size. Like most other health clubs, the gym where I trained had its share of steroid users. I had heard about these drugs but was afraid to take them because of their negative side effects. But knowing I would soon be going to school with guys who were bigger and stronger than I made me seriously consider indulging in these artificial muscle stimulants. If I was ever going to get a date in high school, I had to have a great body. After all, I wasn't very good-looking, and I didn't have enough money to buy a new car. The only thing left for me were big muscles. Based on these warped perceptions, I began taking Dianobol and Winstrol. Since I was afraid of needles, I went with oral steroids, at twenty-five dollars a bottle.

By the time tenth grade began, I was actively pursuing my career in the carpet-cleaning industry and persistently taking steroids to improve my body. However, I soon realized that my attempts to get noticed were failing. The athletes and the guys with the new cars had all the girls. To make matters worse, my two best friends at the time had brand-new trucks that their parents had bought for them, while I was driving a ten-year-old Buick.

At Cleveland High School, Friday night was the most exciting night of the week. All my friends would go to the football or basketball games, but these activities made me feel the most out of place. One night in particular comes to mind. It was the 1982–83 basketball playoffs, and we had a home game that everyone attended. Not wanting to be left out, I also went to the game. There I was, the guy who so desperately wanted to be the center of attention, sitting among hundreds of people, watching somebody else on stage. And what a stage it was with all the fans and those gorgeous cheerleaders entertaining the crowd. I was deeply in love with three of them—anonymously, of course.

We had an outstanding team that year and whenever one of our players made a basket, the entire audience leaped to their feet yelling, screaming, and cheering them on. If you've ever attended a professional sporting event, you know the feeling that comes over you when your team hits a home run, makes a touchdown, or sinks a basket. That's what it was like for everyone in that crowd—except me. I was so envious that the players were getting all the attention—and I wasn't—that I became very angry. The euphoria of the game gave way to a sick feeling of jealousy that inspired me to stop at nothing to get that crowd to cheer for me one day.

The worst part of the game came during the singing of the

fight song. When the band struck up the tune, we stood, pointed to the other team and their fans, and sang:

> Hey tell your mama,
> Hey tell your daddy . . .
> You can't compete with the *Land!*

Get it? Cleve*land?*! A silly song, true, but imagine the excitement and emotion—and volume—as a packed house sang it over and over again in a close, confined gymnasium. While everyone else joined in, I observed the crowd's reaction and thought how I might someday attain such recognition. It was at this game, singing this song, that I realized that there was something different about Barry Minkow: I just couldn't stand to watch an event that wasn't focusing on me. All right, maybe I couldn't outclass my peers in basketball, football, or even baseball, but there was something out there that I could do better than all of them. And it was my goal to find out just what that "something" was.

My worst fear about high school was becoming a reality. I was just another student at Cleveland High School, with no special talents that set me apart from the crowd. I was about to be overcome by that dread disease known as *mediocrity.* Out of sheer desperation for attention, I decided it was time for another fraud.

While at the gym doing squats, I fell forward with 275 pounds on my back and faked a neck injury. I was hospitalized immediately, and all my family and friends came to my bedside, giving me much-needed attention and sympathy. Although it was only temporary, this "injury" provided a built-in excuse for not competing in athletics. It also gave me a potentially great comeback story. I sat in the hospital, imagining how I would tell everyone about my neck injury and the ordeal involved in overcoming this tragic setback.

The biggest task was to fool the neurosurgeon, or at least to convince him that my injury was indeed severe. To do this, I insisted that I had no feeling in my right arm. And since nerve damage is a common result of many neck injuries, my story was believable. Nonetheless, it wasn't easy to perpetrate because of the tests the doctors used to investigate the damage. One in particular required me to tell the doctor that I had no sensation when he rolled a sharp metal object across my arm. But, at that time in my life, the pain was a small price to pay for the attention I was receiving.

Unfortunately, it didn't last. After spending nearly three weeks in the hospital, the doctor released me and told me to stay home from school for an additional four weeks. Not only was I falling behind in my studies, but I also was not working out or participating in social activities. As the novelty of the neck injury wore off, it wasn't long before feelings of loneliness and depression overwhelmed me. I realized it was time to start weight training again and to face high school with a fresh approach. Although the fake injury didn't provide the satisfaction I'd hoped for, at least I'd conned a neurosurgeon and built up confidence in my lying.

By the time tenth grade came to a close, I was miserable. I had nothing to look forward to but another long summer of cleaning carpets and lifting weights, while my friends would spend time with their girlfriends. *Life just isn't fair,* I thought. To combat this emotional depression, I continued my steroid consumption.

Steroid cycles were supposed to last for eight weeks: six weeks of intake followed by a two-week break. The problem was that during these two-week rest periods, I became extremely weak and lost a lot of weight. With things going as poorly as they were, I couldn't handle the comments from people who noticed my weight loss and drop in strength. So I decided to ignore the steroid break periods.

That summer I got a better offer and started working for another company cleaning carpets during the day and phone soliciting at night. These long hours helped me learn how a carpet-cleaning company operates. I dispatched jobs, took new customer orders, and even gave bids on commercial work. Again, I was the youngest employee and enjoyed being surrounded by older people. They respected and admired my commitment to the company and never saw through my insecurities. Did I have them fooled! I remember coming into the office early one Saturday morning and bragging to all the guys about the date I had the night before. Little did they know that my "date" was with my television set.

I was determined that my eleventh-grade year wouldn't end up like the previous one. My body was bigger and stronger than ever as the steroids really began to kick in. This year, Cleveland High was going to know who Barry Minkow was. But as the fall semester began, I again found myself backed against the ropes, taking the everyday problems of high school life "on the chin" and absorbing the body blows of loneliness, depression, and guilt. There didn't seem to be anyone I could talk to about my true feelings. In the eyes of my family and friends, I was an overachiever. I went to school, worked, and lifted weights almost daily. I appeared to have it all together, but in reality I was still searching for something that would satisfy my insatiable desire to be the center of attention. I concluded that I was failing high school, maybe not academically, but definitely socially and emotionally.

Additionally, money problems continued to cause family arguments and dissension at home. But I masked this well and, because I now worked year-round, I helped my family financially whenever possible.

During this low period in my life, two men I had met at the gym impacted me greatly. The first was Jerry Williams, a short but strong weight lifter who always drove an expensive car and paid for everything in cash. Officially, he was a wholesale plumbing distributor. He also (much more discreetly) made usurious loans to businesses and handled bets on the side for his associates. In my eyes he had it all, and I looked up to him because of his wealth, strength, and independence.

The other man was Gary Todd. Although not as strong or well-to-do as Jerry, he was like the older brother I never had. He remembered the days when I had first joined the health club—how I had cleaned the showers to help finance my membership—and was impressed by my determination. He was easy to talk to, and I told him about my problems at school and at home.

Gary often took me out for meals, and we would talk for hours. He was there when I needed him, and I valued our friendship greatly.

❖ ❖ ❖

The sign in the gym read: "Power Lifting Meet—All Ages and Weight Classes Welcome." As I stared at the advertisement, I pictured myself on stage in front of hundreds of people, winning this contest. This is exactly what my ego needed—a victory. Impressed by my dramatic increase in strength over the past twelve months, many at the gym encouraged me to enter the meet, though most were unaware of my steroid abuse.

I went on a six-week, high-intensity strength cycle designed to improve my bench press, squat, and deadlift—the three lifts required of each participant. With the contest only weeks away, I trained long and hard—realizing that this was the only shot I had at being the best at something. I even increased my steroid intake, hoping to give myself a greater advantage.

Convinced that this would be the event that "put Barry Minkow on the map," both in the gym and at school, I bragged to all my friends, promising victory and predicting future participation in even bigger meets.

I left for San Francisco—the site of the meet—vowing to everyone that I would not return without a first-place trophy. But as soon as I stepped into the auditorium, I knew it wasn't going to happen. Hundreds of experienced weight lifters, many of whom had worked out for years, showed up to compete. I hid in the corner of the auditorium, hoping to escape notice as I watched my competitors in the 165-pound weight class lift hundreds of pounds more than I even dreamed of putting on the bar. Because I had entered, I was forced to embarrass myself by performing my lifts.

When the meet ended, I didn't even place in the top ten. Even though I had cheated by taking steroids, I had still lost. The ride home was a long and painful exercise of thinking up lies and excuses for not bringing home a trophy. Not only were my dreams of becoming a world-class power lifter shattered, but I was trapped once again in a world where other people were winning—and I wasn't.

A Chance to Be Zhe Best | 4

J erry Williams had been bugging me for weeks to clean his carpets. Since I had finished my workout and had the equipment in the back of my Buick, I followed him from the gym to his house on what proved to be a fateful evening in the fall of 1982. I had just about recovered from my recent embarrassment at the weight-lifting contest and, as I pulled into Jerry's driveway, my mind was focused on the everyday concerns that the average eleventh-grade student encounters.

Spending time with Jerry Williams away from the gym was a real thrill. He seemed to have it all—money, nice cars, plenty of friends, and lots of workout equipment. Yet despite being twice my age, he always had time for me and was impressed with my dedication to work and weight lifting.

Although his living-room carpet was heavily soiled, I was able to get most of the spots out and actually made it look good. This impressed Jerry. Then, out of nowhere, he asked me how much the equipment I was using would cost to buy new.

"This stuff would cost at least a thousand dollars new at the supply house," I said, thinking he probably wanted his own machine for the next time his carpets got dirty.

"So the equipment you're using now belongs to the company you work for?"

"That's right. They set up the appointments through telephone soliciting and then send me and other carpet cleaners out to do the work."

"I take it the other men are older than you," he joked, then sobered. "Say, Barry, didn't you start off in the phone room, soliciting people and setting up leads?"

Because Jerry didn't know about the phony leads I had set up at Carpets Clean, I felt safe in answering, "That's right, Jerry. And then I went out into the field as a carpet cleaner's helper, got trained, and now I go out on my own."

Jerry smiled, nodded his head, and asked me to sit with him on the couch. "Barry, if you had your own equipment, would you be able to make more money?"

Could he be serious? Was he actually considering spending over a thousand dollars on carpet-cleaning equipment and supplies, for me?

I stumbled through my response. "Of-of course. In fact, if I had my own equipment, I could start my own company. I already know the business inside and out."

Jerry leaned back against the sofa, crossed his legs, and surveyed his clean living-room carpet one last time. "Well, Barry, if you'll give me a price list and description of all the supplies you'll need, I'll front you the money to start your own business."

I could barely contain my excitement. While my mom and dad struggled to pay the phone bill, I was about to be handed a fortune! "Are you serious?"

"Of course I am. But in return I'll want you to pay me back two hundred dollars a week—interest only. Can you earn enough money to support that kind of payment?"

Wow! This was the answer to all my problems. *Nobody at Cleveland High School has their own business,* I thought. I would be the first, and that meant that everybody—including the girls— would have to notice me. Who would remember Barry Minkow, failed weight lifter, when they had Barry Minkow, businessman, to reckon with?

Jerry jarred me from my dream world. "Well, can you earn that kind of money, kid?"

"You bet I can! I'll earn that and a whole lot more," I boasted, not considering the seriousness of such a commitment.

Jerry smiled. "Great. Give me a call tomorrow and let me know how much money you'll need. I'll write you a check and we'll be in business."

"Do you want me to sign some kind of loan papers?" I asked.

Slapping me on the leg, Jerry stood up and said, "Don't be silly, Barry. If I didn't trust you, I wouldn't lend you the money. . . . By the way, the first job for your new company will be to finish my house. Now get busy."

Pumped with adrenaline and relishing the attention and acceptance I would reap from my new business venture, I completed the job in record time.

On my way home I thought about a name for my new company. Since I was constantly driven in my life to be *the best* at something, I decided to call the company "The Best." I couldn't wait to tell Mom and Dad and the guys at work about my new business.

However, my parents were skeptical about Jerry's motives. "Why would a grown man lend some sixteen-year-old kid money to start a business?" Dad protested.

"Because he trusts me!" I answered.

After about an hour of arguing, I convinced my parents that the worst thing that could happen—even if I failed—was that they would get a clean garage out of the deal, as their garage was to be the office for the business.

I had trouble sleeping that Thursday night as I contemplated the tasks I needed to accomplish the next day—clean the garage, get a phone line installed, obtain a business permit (whatever that meant), have some business cards printed, get prices on the equipment I would need, and open my first-ever checking account. I was raring to get started. But first I had to spend part of my day in school.

Early the next morning, before school, I stopped by where I worked to tell my fellow carpet cleaners about "The Best" and the friend at the gym who was financing me. Surprisingly, they were not impressed. I suspect they felt they deserved a chance at their own business more than I did.

Before I left, a fellow worker jokingly said, "Why don't you call the company 'Z-Best' instead of 'The Best'? It has a better ring to it."

As I drove to school, I decided that ZZZZ Best, with four Zs (because I wanted four kids someday), would be the name of the company. But as I spread the news around Cleveland High that Friday, most of my contemporaries laughed at me. Like my failure in weight lifting, they viewed this as another vain attempt on my part to break from the monotony of my life. I left school that day determined to prove them wrong.

❖ ❖ ❖

It didn't take me long to arrive at the start-up figure of $1,600. That included the purchase of a steam cleaner, a shampooer, some carpet-repair tools, and such miscellaneous expenses as printing costs, licensing, and phone installation. Jerry Williams was faithful to his word.

After cashing the check at a bank in Van Nuys, I headed for the offices of the *Northridger,* which published DBA (doing business as) notices for new companies.

"And what's the official name of this new business, Mr. Minkow?" asked the lady who sat behind the loan desk.

"ZZZZ Best Carpet-and-Furniture-Cleaning Company," I replied proudly.

"And are you the sole owner, or do you have a partner?"

Jerry had said nothing about a partnership. I was in charge, as long as I paid him the two hundred dollars per week. I didn't want to answer to or be a partner with anyone. I wanted the glory all to myself. "No, ma'am, I'm the sole owner."

"Do you have any identification?" she asked. I pulled my driver's license from my wallet and set it on the desk. She looked at it once, began to type and then stopped, grabbed the license, and inspected it more closely. "You were born in 1966?"

"Yes, ma'am," I responded confidently. "Is that a problem?"

"I don't know. I've never opened·a business for a sixteen-year-old kid before. Are you still in high school?"

"I'm in eleventh grade at Cleveland High."

She smiled, looked at me and the license once more, and then gave it back to me. "I don't know of any law preventing me from doing this. Do you have the forty-five-dollar fee?"

"You bet I do!" I handed it over and within fifteen minutes the process was completed.

As I got ready to leave, the nice lady said, "Good luck, Mr. Minkow. I wish more kids your age would start their own business." She paused and then continued, "Who knows, maybe you'll open the door for others."

I thanked her, but paid little attention to what she had said. *Who cares about others?* I thought. I was doing this solely for my own benefit.

With the DBA in hand, my next stop was a local bank. I sat down at the new accounts desk and explained that I wanted to open a business checking account. Although surprised that I was only sixteen, the clerk gladly opened the account and supplied me with temporary checks.

With my new status as a businessman, I quickly joined the Chamber of Commerce, got a business phone installed in the garage, bought materials, and paid the printer for the first five hundred ZZZZ Best business cards.

Then I shifted my attention to obtaining customers. All the equipment in the world meant nothing unless I had carpets to clean. From my experience at the two carpet-cleaning companies, I knew the most cost-effective way of getting a lot of business fast was telephone soliciting. But since I was stuck at school every weekday from 7:30 A.M. until 1:00 P.M., I couldn't do the telephoning. So I hired the best solicitor I had ever known—my mother. She would set up leads during the day and, when I got home from school, I would go out with a helper and do the work.

She agreed to work for $225 a week. Because I had a few hundred dollars in reserve, I didn't mind committing to the expense. Besides, she could generate enough business to pay her own way almost immediately.

Two weeks later, I sat behind my garage desk, put my feet up, and reflected on what I had just accomplished. While most of my friends at school were wrapped up in upcoming geometry tests and acne breakouts and the mundane routine of high school life, I was the sole owner of my very own business. I had done something that many twice my age would only dream of doing. I picked up a ZZZZ Best business card, stared at it, and thought about Mindy Jamison. She was the twelfth-grade cheerleader with whom I was deeply in love. To her, I was just another high school junior—but ZZZZ Best was going to change that. One day soon she was going to know that Barry Minkow was someone special.

❖ ❖ ❖

My victory party ended with a call from the bank. They informed me that because I was under eighteen, I was not allowed to sign any legally binding contract, including checks. Consequently, they had closed my account and bounced all my checks.

Within days, the supply house, the printer, and even the Reseda Chamber of Commerce called demanding payments. Unfortunately, they called when I was at school, and my mom had to field their complaints. She worried that I was headed for failure.

Then there was Jerry Williams. The man who just weeks before had funded my new company quickly lost confidence in me when two of my checks to him bounced. He wanted his money! Plus, I had payday coming up, and then the phone bill. The clincher came when two large carpet-cleaning appointments, worth almost four hundred dollars, postponed to another month. I had to think of something—fast!

First, I needed to open another checking account. There had to be one bank out there that would give a sixteen-year-old carpet cleaner a chance. I was determined to find it, and I did. A suburban branch opened the account for me. To appear more businesslike, I wore a suit, hoping they wouldn't notice the age on my driver's license. If they didn't ask my age, I wasn't about to tell them. It worked, and I was on my way—with temporary checks in hand—making payments to those I owed. I had to convince many of them to take another check, but after assuring them that I had my problems straightened out, they gave me another chance.

With the bill collectors temporarily out of the way, I got on the phones to do what I did best—drum up business. It took me less than four hours to replace the customers who had postponed. And I didn't stop there. To pay Williams and the other expenses, I needed more business and additional crews out in the field while I was at school. I immediately hired Vera Hojecki, a long-time solicitor friend of my mother. After I put in another phone line, the two teamed up and more than doubled our business.

I also hired Mike McGee to work with a partner out in the field. He was a great carpet cleaner (much better and more experienced than I), and he could do carpet-repair work. I had known him since I was a kid, and was surprised that he agreed to work for me. But he knew of Vera's and my mom's ability to create business, and that, more than anything else, sold him on the company.

Although balancing ZZZZ Best with school was difficult, I was more than holding my own. I was learning how to deal with all kinds of people—customers, angry suppliers, and employees—and this increased my ability to sell. And to manipulate.

But just as I was beginning to think that I had finally made it over the proverbial hump, I got another phone call. The branch bank manager where I had my checking account wanted to see me.

❖　❖　❖

"We're really sorry, Mr. Minkow, but we have to close your account. California law states that you must be eighteen years of age to open a checking account." The bank manager put out his hand and I shook it. "Come back in two years, and we'll be glad to open a business account for ZZZZ Best."

"Are you going to bounce the checks I've already written on the account?" I asked, trying to restrain the note of pleading in my voice.

"I'm afraid so, son, but instead of stamping them 'Insufficient Funds,' we'll put 'Account Closed' on each check."

"That's decent of you!" I burst out sarcastically. I felt I had a right to be mad. This was the second bank that had closed my checking account in the past month. "No wonder kids my age don't go into business more often. You banks won't give us a chance."

"I know you're frustrated, Mr. Minkow. And to be honest with you, if it was in my power, I'd keep your account open because I admire what you're doing." He walked around his large mahogany desk and put his hand on my shoulder. "I wish I'd had your ambition when I was sixteen."

It wasn't that I didn't appreciate his compliments, but I had outstanding checks that were about to bounce—*again!* I thought about the Chamber of Commerce and my four employees. And about the supply house. I had sworn that the ninety-seven-dollar check I had written them was good. Now they'd never take another check from me.

I looked down and rubbed the back of my neck. I was confused, and the pressure on me was mounting. "Looks like you guys need your carpets cleaned," I joked. "I know of a good company, but I hear they only take cash."

He laughed, and we said our good-byes. *Who knows,* I thought, *maybe I'll come back in two years and open an account with him.* I left the bank, trying to sort out in my sixteen-year-old mind how I was going to handle these financial difficulties.

As I drove back to the garage-office, I thought about quitting. Who needed all this rejection anyway? Although I despised mediocrity, it did have certain advantages. Before ZZZZ Best, I may have been lonely, but at least I didn't have the pressure of payroll! If I closed the company, only Mom, Mike, Vera, and one other person would be affected. But then I remembered Mindy Jamison. If I was going to get her (or some other beautiful girl) to notice me, I had to keep the company open so I could earn enough money to buy a new car. Then, and only then, could I ask her out. And if she said yes, all the aggravation would have been worthwhile.

But before I could buy a new car, I needed to cover my bounced checks and then find a way to cash the checks I received from my customers. Here I was, trying to make an honest living in the business world and getting no cooperation or sympathy from anyone. I was a victim of my age.

The more banks I passed, the angrier I became. *If these guys aren't going to help me, I'll have to figure out some other way to run my business,* I thought. It was this kind of thinking that led me into compromise.

Putting Out Fires | 5

As I mentally surveyed my limited options, I passed a neighborhood convenience store, located a few blocks from the garage-office. A new sign flashed above the store: "Ron's Quick Check Cashing." I pulled into the parking lot and walked into the back room where I knew I would find Ron, the owner.

"Barry! How are you, my friend?" he greeted me.

Ron was a family friend who put in long hours at the store and had single-handedly built it from nothing to a successful business. Many times, as a youngster, I had helped him stock the shelves. The pay was always the same—one six-pack of Hostess minidonuts (chocolate, of course) and a can of cola. Even if there was no work when I showed up, he would create some easy task to justify giving me the free food. Ron was a good man and a better friend.

"I'm okay, Ron, but I have a small problem." We shook hands and he guided me to the cage where the soda pop was stored. We pulled up two crates and sat down.

"How's the carpet-cleaning business coming?" he asked.

I paused before answering and took note of the many boxes of inventory. I had seen this stuff a thousand times, but now that I was in business, it had taken on a different meaning. They were no longer just boxes, but dollars and cents. Ron was making big bucks, and I wished I were in his shoes.

"To be honest with you, I'm having trouble keeping a checking account open," I confessed. "It seems that until I'm eighteen years old, I'm not allowed to sign any legally binding contracts. So I can't write checks or deposit my customers' checks." I paused and lowered my voice. "Basically, Ron, I'm out of business."

"Why don't you get your dad to cosign on the account for you? I'm sure he'd be happy to do it."

I thought back to the question the lady at the *Northridger* had asked me: "Do you have any partners?" ZZZZ Best may not have been much, but it was 100 percent mine! "Ron, this is my company! I've worked hard to get it started, and I want to keep it. If I'm dependent on my dad or anyone to sign checks for me, it really isn't my business anymore. Do you know what I mean?"

"Sure I do, kid." He smiled. "I'll tell you what I'll do for you. Just bring me your customer checks, and I'll cash them for you. If you need to pay a bill or something, I'll give you a money order made out to whoever you want. This way you can keep control of your business."

The idea sounded too good to be true. I squinted at him. "How much will you charge me for each check?"

"The normal fee for the check-cashing business is 5 percent of the face amount of the check. But for you, I'll lower it to 3 percent. Does that sound fair?"

"It sure does!" I exclaimed, and wondered how I could repay such a favor. "Can I do anything for you in return?"

"Well, my carpets at the house are pretty dirty. Do you think you can take care of them for me?"

"Say no more!" I interjected. "I'll personally go out and clean them for you. How about Saturday morning?"

"That would be great. I wanted to have them cleaned before the holidays." He got up as the buzzer announced the arrival of a customer up front. "In the meantime, just come by whenever you need to cash some checks. I'll let my staff know about our special arrangement."

I rose and shook Ron's hand, feeling a weight roll off my chest, and left the store with a whole new outlook on life. *Who needs those stupid banks anyway?* I thought.

I drove home as fast as I could and pulled into the driveway. Mom and Vera were on the phones in the garage. I marched into the temporary office and asked my usual question, "How many leads did you guys get?"

Both of them smiled, a signal that generally meant business was good. And considering that I was paying each of them $225 a week, I expected production.

"Any calls?" I asked.

"Just Jerry," Vera said. "He was a little upset because the two-hundred-dollar check you gave him bounced."

"Don't worry, I'll call him back. And there won't be any more bounced checks around here. I just made a deal with Ron at the store to get money orders in exchange for customer checks. No longer am I dependent on these bankers."

"That's great, Barry," Mom replied, hoping that what I said was true. The calls from all the angry people with the bounced checks were getting to her. "That will save you a lot of time."

I got comfortable in my chair before I picked up the phone to call Jerry. "Jerry, this is Barry. Look, I'm sorry that check bounced, but I've got some good—"

"I don't want to hear it, Barry," he cut me off angrily. "My bank won't take any more of your checks." He was furious. "Every week you come up with some excuse about why you can't pay me, and I always let you off the hook. But now you owe me eight hundred dollars, and I need the money! I'm running a business, too, and I can't afford to let you slip through the cracks every week."

There was no way I could get anywhere with this angry man over the phone. My brief experience in business had taught me the benefits of persuading with eye-to-eye contact. "Are you going to be at home for a while?" I asked.

"Yeah, I'll be here for another hour or so."

"I'll be there in twenty minutes." I hung up and raced to my car. *Another fire to put out,* I thought. "I'll be back in an hour!" I yelled to my mother. "Take my messages."

I was certainly getting a crash course in crisis management. I needed to make some kind of arrangement with Jerry, because if I gave him the eight hundred dollars all at once, I wouldn't be able to meet payroll. Besides, he shouldn't have charged interest for my first two weeks in business, because I had spent most of that time organizing, not earning income.

Within fifteen minutes I was pulling into Jerry's driveway. As I knocked on his door, I wondered how much money he was actually making in the plumbing supply business. He always carried around a lot of cash neatly folded in his pocket and everyone, including me, seemed to owe him money. I wished I were in such a position.

"Come on in, Barry," Jerry called from his usual spot on the end of a large sofa. He was writing checks from his business checking account.

It must be nice to be able to write checks, I thought. I sat down at the other end of the couch.

"What's the excuse this time?" he asked.

"The bank closed my account again. They found out I was only sixteen years old."

"Why did they let you open the account in the first place?" he snapped.

"I don't know. I guess they didn't suspect that anyone under eighteen years of age would need a business account. And based on what I've been through these past several weeks, I can see why." I was relieved when he smiled—almost laughed. "But don't worry, Jerry. I've made a deal with a check-cashing place near my house. They're going to cash all my customer checks for a 3 percent fee and give me money orders in return. And you know that a money order can't bounce."

"That's great. But what about the eight hundred you owe me? I've got to give a guy a big loan, and it's going to make me short."

I wonder how much weekly interest he has to pay? I said to myself. I was certain that my presentation about the money orders would buy me some time with him. But now he was in need, and there could be no more delays.

Regardless, I gave it one more try. "If you give me a few weeks, I can catch up. Mom and Vera have set up some big jobs that I'll be doing personally, so I can keep all the proceeds. Meanwhile, I've got payroll in three days and an overdue phone bill." A glance at Jerry told me he wasn't buying it.

"Why is it that I'm always last on your priority list, Barry?" he complained. "Without me, you wouldn't even have a company!"

Jerry wasn't the kind of guy I wanted to rile. Even though I was on steroids and fairly strong, he was much bigger and a lot more intimidating.

"I know, Jerry, and I'm not trying to jerk you around, but it's just that I'm hurting right now. I can't walk into a bank like a normal businessman and get a loan when cash is short. I don't have that option. In fact, I can't even open a checking account!"

He listened attentively—a good sign. Then he said, "I'll tell you what I'll do. Come back tomorrow with five hundred dollars in cash or money orders. I'll let the other three hundred ride until after the first of the year. But that's the best I can do for you." He looked at me, awaiting a response.

Although I couldn't afford the five hundred, it was the best deal I was going to get. "That's fine, Jerry. I'll see you tomorrow about two o'clock. If I'm a little late, don't worry. I get out of school at one, and from there I'll need to go to the convenience store."

"No problem. I'll see you at two, or close to it."

I got up, shook his hand in defeat, and left the house. On

the way home, I thought about how I was going to juggle my funds in order to meet my many obligations. If I gave Jerry five hundred, that would leave me with only six hundred to cover payroll and the phone bill. But those expenses totaled close to a thousand dollars. I was in trouble. Where would I come up with the other four hundred dollars?

The good news was that this was Tuesday, and I had until Friday—payday—to figure it all out. Maybe I could generate enough business on Wednesday and Thursday to cover the four hundred. But because I was in school, Mike and his partner had to do all the cleaning. Since I paid them 50 percent of whatever they brought in, this took a big bite out of my profit. *When will I start making money?* I wondered.

When I arrived at the garage-office I asked my mom and Vera if there were any calls.

"Just one. The supply store called and said the check that you swore wouldn't bounce, did. They want one hundred fifteen dollars in cash no later than Friday."

I moaned. "Great! I'm falling in love with today." I plopped into my chair and rubbed my tired eyes. "Don't worry, Mom, I'll straighten out this mess." It was difficult to keep up company morale when every two hours, someone was yelling about a bounced check. But that was a price I had to pay if I wanted the fame and glory that came with running my own business at the age of sixteen.

❖   ❖   ❖

I gathered the checks from the past two days and, after making a few phone calls, dashed out of the garage and headed to my new "bank." At the convenience store I would get money to pay Jerry and the carpet supplies store.

The buzzer sounded its usual warning as I went through the door. As a youngster, I had passed through this door maybe a thousand times. I remembered back to those summer days when my sister Sheri and I would walk barefoot to Ron's Convenience Store, buy some candy and soda pop, and play hide-and-seek for the rest of the day. Back then I wasn't worried about things like payroll, supplies, or Jerry Williams. Maybe ZZZZ Best was forcing me to grow up too quickly.

Ron's voice woke me from my daydream. "Come on over here, Barry. Let's see how much you got for me."

"A little over six hundred," I replied, waving the checks.

Ron opened a drawer and took out a small box containing several blank money orders. He also pulled out a small machine with a handle attached to it. Adjusting the numbers on the machine, Ron inserted the money orders, one after another, pulling the handle for each. And then, much to my surprise, he simply initialed the bottom of each money order, pulled off his copy, and handed me the blank original.

"Don't you have to fill these out?" I asked.

"No, I only imprint and initial the money order. You fill in the 'pay to the order of' section on the top." He pointed to it, and I filled it in.

Then I endorsed the back of my customer checks, gave them to Ron, and was ready to go.

"Can you wait here a minute, Barry? I need to get my logbook in the back so I can record this transaction."

"Go ahead, pal. I've got a minute."

He walked to the back of the store—out of sight—while I leaned against the counter next to the cash register, wondering again how I was going to cover this Friday's payroll. I looked down at my three money orders and then, out of the corner of my eye, I noticed the small box of blank money orders. There, within easy reach, lay the solution to all my problems. If I took just two of them and quickly stamped in two hundred dollars on each, I would be home free.

I surveyed the store. It was empty. Outside, the busy sidewalk gave way to a street filled with traffic. Rationalizations and justifications flooded my thinking: *I have people depending on me for payroll. It's not like I'll steal the money and go buy drugs. I'd be stealing for a good cause. Besides, no one is giving me a chance. It's not my fault that the banks keep closing my accounts, causing me to pay service charges on each returned check. I'll figure out some way to pay Ron back. He'll understand. Even if I get caught, I won't get in trouble because I'm just a kid trying to run a business.*

I looked at the money orders again, then at the imprinting machine. Ron was still gone. I thought about the embarrassment of failure. The last thing I wanted was to go out of business and have everybody think I was a flop—again! One final look. No customers, no Ron.

I grabbed two blank money orders from the bottom of the box. By the time Ron noticed, I'd have paid him back. I pulled the machine around, set it for two hundred dollars, inserted the money order, and nervously pulled down the handle. It barely made any noise. Before I put the second money order in, I looked around again. I pulled the handle. What seemed like an eternity really only took minutes.

Quickly I slid the money orders into my pocket, put the machine back neatly with the handle facing away from me, and made sure the box of money orders was in its original place. *This is a lot more serious than setting up phony leads at Carpets Clean,* I thought. I had actually committed my first real crime!

"Sorry I took so long, Barry. It seems my wife took the logbook home with her." Ron walked to his position in front of the cash register. "But that's okay. Need anything else?"

"No, Ron," I said, hoping I didn't look or sound suspicious. "I'll probably be back tomorrow if that's okay?"

"That'll be great," he said as I turned toward the door. "Oh, Barry . . . don't forget Saturday morning."

A cold chill crawled down my spine. This was my friend! He had helped me when nobody else would, and I had just stolen four hundred dollars from him. Now I was going to his house to clean carpets! Stealing from Ron was a mistake, but it had to be done. I had no other option . . . or so I thought.

"I'll be there at nine o'clock, my friend."

PART 2:
Corruption

Compromise Becomes Corruption | 6

After the incident at Ron's store, there was no turning back. I had crossed the line of legitimacy, and I was determined to do whatever it took to keep ZZZZ Best going, even if that meant committing another crime. My 1983 New Year's resolution consisted of two words: "Add fame." Sure, some of the students at Cleveland High knew I had started my own company, but I wasn't getting nearly the recognition I thought I deserved. To solve this problem (and to increase sales), I created my own publicity.

I had noticed that the many different people I met while cleaning carpets after school and on weekends all reacted to me the same way. They were always impressed, and sometimes overwhelmed, by the fact that, at age sixteen, I was the owner of a company. I used this human-interest angle to generate new business. For example, when I walked into a house to clean only the living room, I would get to know the customer, tell my success story, and end up cleaning the whole house. In some cases I quadrupled the price of the original job.

One day, while I was alone in the garage-office, I called Channel 4 News in Los Angeles. Disguising my voice to sound older, I told a segment producer that I had just had my carpets cleaned by the sixteen-year-old owner of ZZZZ Best Carpet-and-Furniture-Cleaning Company, and I was most impressed by the fact that a high school junior was running his own business.

"Why is it that we always hear stories about teenage drug users and dropouts but never hear success stories like this?" I questioned him. "What could be a better model for other young people than a guy who has defied the odds and started his own company?" The producer was soon convinced that the story was newsworthy, even inspirational. I gave him the company phone number so he could set up an interview with this young entrepreneur. Then I hung up and sat back to wait.

In less than five minutes, the phone rang. "I'm trying to reach a Mr. Barry Minkow," said the male caller.

"Who may I say is calling?" As if I didn't know.

"Tell him Channel 4 News is interested in doing a profile on his carpet-cleaning company."

Within days a film crew was in my garage, shooting ZZZZ Best in action. The story aired that evening, and the response was incredible. Radio stations, the *Daily News,* and even my school newspaper called, wanting interviews. Prospective customers called, demanding that Barry Minkow *personally* clean their carpets. At school, I was no longer viewed as a failure who only dreamed of success, but as the *only* student at Cleveland High publicly recognized as a businessman. Even Mindy Jamison and some of the other pretty girls acknowledged my success.

All this fame helped numb the feelings of guilt that had arisen from stealing Ron's money orders. Somehow fame erased pain— at least temporarily.

As my income increased during the spring of 1983, I found it more and more difficult to run the company without a checking account. So, attempting to capitalize on my recent notoriety, I searched for a bank that would accept my business. Rather than trying to con them up front by withholding my age, I looked for a banker who would so identify with the human-interest side of the ZZZZ Best story that he or she would ignore the minimum-age law and give me a chance. It was during this search that I met Doug Fitzgerald, at Town Bank in a nearby suburb.

A smart man with many years in banking and a keen mind for business, Doug agreed to open a business checking account for me if I promised to discuss ZZZZ Best progress with him at least three times weekly. In addition to Town Bank, Jerry Williams also used his influence at Second Savings, and I opened a checking account there as well.

To handle the extra business and stay ahead of my many expenses, I hired additional telephone solicitors to work in the evenings and another carpet-cleaning crew. But Jerry's two-hundred-dollar weekly payment, the payrolls, and other expenses caught up with me, and I faced yet another financial crisis.

To make matters worse, Ron called, having traced his missing money orders to me. "How could you steal from me, Barry?" he ranted. "I was there for you when nobody else was! I just can't believe it!"

Although I vehemently denied any wrongdoing, he knew better and demanded his money.

If I can just hang on until school gets out, I'll be able to fix all these problems, I thought. Since I could do most of the jobs myself, my profit margin would double and I'd climb out of debt—if I could survive until June.

After Ron's call, I sat at my garage desk and developed a plan of action. I checked the balance in my checkbooks from Town Bank and Second Savings and realized that I was almost twelve hundred dollars short. "I just can't get ahead!" I yelled as I slammed my fist against the desk. Just then I came across a slip of paper from Town Bank that showed my current account balance. It was higher than what the checkbook revealed—presumably because some of the checks I had written had not yet cleared. I picked up my Second Savings checkbook and wondered how long it would take for a check deposited at Town Bank to make it back to Second Savings. *At least a couple of days,* I thought, *and definitely long enough for me to meet the payroll.* Within minutes I was on my way to Town Bank.

"Why are you depositing a check from one ZZZZ Best account to another?" an officer at Town Bank asked.

"Just transferring some funds," I said confidently. "Anything wrong with that?"

"No, Barry. Not at all. I just wanted to make sure there was no check kiting going on. . . . It's my job." She initialed her approval on the deposit slip.

So that's the official name of my crime, I said to myself on the way back from the bank. *I'm a check kiter!*

❖   ❖   ❖

That weekend I worried about how long it would take for that check to hit Second Savings. If it bounced and Jerry found out, I'd be in big trouble. Not only would I have Ron after me, but Jerry and Doug Fitzgerald as well. I had to cover that check!

That Sunday afternoon, my Grandma came over. Although preoccupied with my problems, I enjoyed seeing her. Grandma had always encouraged me with my business endeavor, was proud of ZZZZ Best, and made it a point to tell her friends about me. In fact, shortly after I started the company, she had loaned me money to buy additional equipment. But when I greeted her on that hot spring afternoon, she was upset because she had forgotten to bring a package from her West Hollywood apartment.

"No problem, Grandma. Give me the keys to your place, and I'll drive over and pick it up for you."

After some convincing, she relented, and I was on my way to her apartment. As I drove past the many businesses along the streets of the San Fernando Valley, I wondered how many of them were worried about big interest payments and bounced checks. Although I couldn't answer that question, I did know that ZZZZ Best had earned me respect in the eyes of everyone—and thus I couldn't let it fail. That's when I saw a sign that read: "Jewelry Exchange—Cash for All Kinds of Jewelry."

Then I remembered Grandma's jewelry. She kept it in her bedroom, in a dresser drawer beneath a large wall mirror. I had seen it hundreds of times growing up, but this was the first time I had ever contemplated *stealing* some of it. But if I could just take a few pieces and sell them, maybe she wouldn't notice.

When I opened her apartment door, the unforgettable smell of Grandma's perfume pricked my conscience. *I can't steal jewelry from my grandma,* I thought. Then my mind turned to the money orders and the check kiting. *I'm turning into a real crook.* Still, I had people depending on me—not only my employees, but my many contemporaries who now looked up to me. I was becoming a modern hero in the Los Angeles area, and I couldn't let all those people down.

The jewelry was neatly organized in an old box. I dumped it out on the bed and took the most expensive pieces. Then I covered my tracks by returning the remaining pieces to their original places. I put the box back, closed the drawer, grabbed Grandma's package, and sped back to the house. But before going in, I hid the jewelry in my glove compartment.

Grandma greeted my return with a big hug and kiss and profuse thanks for going out of my way to help her. When she left that evening, I was so busy hoping she wouldn't notice the missing jewelry that I forgot to wish her a safe trip home.

After school on Monday, I sold the jewelry. I didn't get the price I should have, but because I needed the funds so desperately, I took what I could get. I covered the check and survived another crisis. I even arranged a settlement plan with Ron.

Every week ZZZZ Best stayed in business, I earned more and more attention and respect. Since I was a provider for the family, my parents found it difficult to discipline and control my behavior. By the time I finished eleventh grade, I had become totally independent.

❖ ❖ ❖

With school in summer recess, I was able to devote 100 percent of my time to ZZZZ Best. During the day I cleaned carpets, and at night I ran the phone room. I slowly pulled my head above water as I caught up with Jerry and made the payrolls.

But then Grandma noticed that her jewelry was missing. Several family members concluded that I had to have taken it. She had worn it just days before I had gone to her apartment, and she hadn't seen it since. They had caught me. But as in the case of Ron's money orders, I denied any wrongdoing.

However, since I feared that news of my crime would spread, I agreed to settle with Grandma quietly for two thousand dollars, the replacement value of the jewelry. Even though this put me behind again, it helped appease my family. But my grandmother never got over the fact that the grandson she loved and helped had betrayed her.

Despite the two-thousand-dollar setback, I decided to move the company from my parents' garage to the two-story Reseda Business Center on Darby Avenue, not far from my house. The Center was leasing industrial office space at very low rates. For three hundred dollars a month, I rented two upstairs offices in a building that housed automotive shops, cabinetmakers, and ironworkers. None were thrilled with the idea of a seventeen-year-old businessman leasing space and having a fleet of carpet-cleaning trucks cruising back and forth in front of their offices, but I didn't care. One day I'd buy the building and throw them all out!

The biggest expense of the move was the phones. Pacific Bell wanted a thousand-dollar deposit to install six telephone lines. After paying out two thousand to Grandma, I didn't have the money and was forced to borrow from Jerry—again! Nonetheless, the thrill of being in charge of a *real* company in a *real* office setting far outweighed the price of Jerry's money.

I hired additional solicitors and cleaners, hoping they would help cover the new expenses. This sudden expansion, along with the move, boosted company morale to an all-time high. I began to hold weekly employee meetings—attendance mandatory. To increase professionalism, I ruled that all cleaners and solicitors— including my mother—refer to me as "Mr. Minkow." I figured that since I had to endure so much as the owner of the company, I was entitled to some respect.

Throughout the summer of 1983, my relationship with Doug Fitzgerald deepened. He advised me to take out business insurance, provide employee incentives, and hire an accountant. I trusted Doug, but not enough to tell him about the check kiting, Grandma's jewelry, and the Ron's Quick-Check incident. After seeing an abundance of checks written to Jerry Williams, Doug inquired as to my relationship with him. I told him that Jerry had lent me some money but was not a partner in the company. He sensed that I wasn't telling the whole story about Jerry, but he never pressed the issue.

As summer came to a close, I was behind financially and deeper in debt. ZZZZ Best existed from payroll to payroll, earning barely enough to cover expenses. And I was still driving an old, beat-up car!

To get the company into a positive cash-flow situation, I reverted to my old check-kiting scheme. But after I let a few checks bounce, the banks were onto me right away. A furious Doug Fitzgerald called me into his office, presented the evidence of my crime, and asked me to explain myself.

As usual, I denied any wrongdoing and blamed the events on the rapid growth of the company. "I'm only seventeen, Doug! I can't keep control of everything." This excuse usually worked with everyone—except Doug!

"Why didn't you tell me you had another active business

checking account at Second Savings? You made me look like an idiot in front of the operations people here!" he yelled. "I talked to the people at Second Savings, and they're closing your account. I should do the same."

He got out of his chair and moved to the end of the desk. Staring me in the eye, he gave me the following warning: "I like you, Barry, and I have a lot of respect for what you've accomplished. But if you're going to make it big in the business world, you're going to need integrity. That means you've got to be honest with your banker. I'm going to let you make payments on the overdraft that you have incurred as a result of the check kiting. But if you do anything like this again, I'll have to close the account." He paused for effect. "You got it, kid?"

"Yes sir, Doug," I said, and putting on my most sincere seventeen-year-old look, I apologized and assured him it wouldn't happen again.

I returned to the office and found Jerry, waiting to yell at me for embarrassing him at his bank. Since they had lost no money, they merely closed my account and swore they'd never do business with ZZZZ Best again. As for Jerry, I denied kiting checks and told him I needed to hire an accountant to take care of the company's funds. He was satisfied with this answer and dropped the issue. I had made it through another crisis! But each time I had to lie, manipulate, and cheat more than the time before, just to achieve the same result.

❖　❖　❖

I returned to Cleveland High School for my senior year as an object of great respect with teachers and students alike. Before then, only the star athletes received recognition, but the success of ZZZZ Best had changed that, putting Barry Minkow in the spotlight—just where I wanted to be. (The only problem was that Mindy Jamison had graduated and wasn't there to see my newfound fame.)

The media continued to hail me as the seventeen-year-old boy genius. And banks and other financial institutions actually called me and solicited my business now. What a change that was! Diner's Club even sent me a credit card, upon which I promptly charged dinners at fancy restaurants for several school friends. In return, I received the satisfaction of watching my one-time critics envy and admire my success. Somehow this made all the lying, cheating, and manipulating worthwhile. When the bill for the credit card came due (almost five thousand dollars), I claimed that the charges were fraudulent and refused to pay. I had developed a pattern of denial that would not soon change.

The demands of running the company and going to school finally took their toll on my workout program. But because my ego wouldn't allow my body to deteriorate, I increased my steroid intake. Instead of just one or two kinds, I now took three simultaneously, hoping to maintain my strength. The cost was high—debilitating pains in my right kidney—but for those of us who yearn to be "zhe best" in everything, it was the price of doing business. I gladly paid it.

But on the business side, it was the same old, same old. The additional employees and the overhead of a real office once again depleted my available cash. I struggled to meet the weekly expenses and missed three or four "Jerry" payments. I was as bad off financially as when I started my business, a year earlier. My inability to retain capital seemed to be the problem. There had to be a better way than scrambling from week to week—and I was determined to find it.

Doug Fitzgerald was happy that I had paid down the overdraft at Town Bank. Back in his good graces, I asked him to approve a business loan for ZZZZ Best. After all, I had been in business for over a year, employed almost twenty people, and had proved that the company could generate consistent income.

But when Doug explained that to qualify for a loan I needed assets, profit-and-loss statements, balance sheets, and the like prepared by an accountant, I was at a loss. Not only did I not have that stuff—I didn't even know what a profit-and-loss statement was!

"Yeah, Doug, but look at these letters from other banks that want my business. Won't they give me a loan?" I asked in desperation.

"No, Barry. They're not going to lower their standards just for you. I can assure you that wherever you apply, you'll see that the requirements will be the same."

I didn't believe him. I left the bank in a huff, swearing that I would find a banker out there who had heard my story and would make ZZZZ Best a loan—without all those financial statements. But Doug was right. I spent most of my Christmas break traipsing from bank to bank and found not one that would bend the rules. Most demanded a three-year track record before one could even be considered for a loan. That was okay, because if *they* wanted to block my legitimate avenues for raising money, I could always turn to some illegitimate avenues.

I determined that no matter what the cost, I needed to open another ZZZZ Best location, to generate more income to help pay the expenses. My goal was to get one location running so well that it would pay the bills for both offices, leaving the income from the other office as pure profit. The cost of another office, I figured, would be ten thousand dollars.

I thought back to the twenty-thousand-dollar insurance policy I had taken out on my carpet-cleaning equipment (well over the actual value). The agent had told me that if the equipment were ever stolen, the company would cut me a check for any amount up to that figure. A plan hatched in my mind. As with the money orders and check kiting, I kept the scheme to myself—trusting no one.

The busy Reseda Business Center had no security to speak

of, and many people had access to the upstairs office space. One afternoon, I waited until my last employee left and then I snuck back into the office and staged a burglary. I pulled out a few drawers, threw away an old upholstery cleaner, relocated some carpet-repair tools, and went home for the evening, leaving my office people to discover the break-in the next morning.

I was sitting in my history class when someone from the office rushed in with an emergency note: "Have Barry Minkow call his office immediately." I relished the intrigue that went with being called out of a high school classroom—with all my friends watching—to attend to the demands of the business world.

On the phone, I instructed my mother to call the police and have them make a report. That way I could quickly substantiate my insurance claim and get the money faster. Within days, an adjuster from my insurance company handed me a draft for the entire amount of my claim—twelve thousand dollars. As I drove to Town Bank to deposit the draft, I thought about how I could explain this large influx of cash to Doug Fitzgerald.

I couldn't tell him I had been burgled of twelve-thousand-dollars worth of equipment, because he had been to the office and knew I didn't have nearly that much stuff. I needed to come up with something else. I remembered that Doug knew that ZZZZ Best had occasionally worked some small, emergency water-damage claims for Trust Insurance. He knew that Gary Todd, my friend from the gym, was an adjuster for Trust, and that he had called on ZZZZ Best more than once to clean carpeting damaged by water or fire. The payments were always made by draft.

I walked into the bank and told Doug that Gary had recommended ZZZZ Best to a friend who was an adjuster for my insurance carrier; that we had been called upon by this new client to perform restoration services on a large building, and that the draft was simply the money we had rightfully earned for services rendered. He believed me. He even gave me immediate credit on the draft, which enabled me to purchase supplies for ZZZZ Best's second location. I had successfully pulled off another crime. Each time it seemed to bother me less.

I located the second office in Thousand Oaks. Although thirty minutes from the Reseda headquarters, the area was booming with new housing and had tremendous potential. News of the expansion did wonders for company morale. No longer were employees worried that their paychecks might bounce. Even suppliers began to take ZZZZ Best seriously. *Maybe 1984 is my year to make it big,* I thought to myself.

If running one office was difficult while going to school, trying to run two was nearly impossible. Instead of struggling to pay twenty people a week, I now had fifty to pay. Plus, I spent many hours traveling back and forth from Thousand Oaks. But with the expansion came increases in power and control. Being the boss of almost fifty employees kept me in constant demand, which helped me feel needed and wanted.

Unfortunately, the Thousand Oaks office lost money because of management problems. To compensate, I moved my mom to the office, along with another employee. They straightened out the problems, but not before my cash was again depleted.

The good news was that the competition had finally begun to take notice. Larger companies, which had for years dominated the industry in the Los Angeles area, were now getting a run for their money—by a seventeen-year-old kid! Our telephone soliciting and prominent yellow-pages ads brought us a substantial volume of business. But, because of my lack of financial experience, we were unable to reap the benefit of these large gross sales.

❖ ❖ ❖

As my eighteenth birthday approached in March of 1984, my parents were concerned about my college plans. Before I started ZZZZ Best, it had always been my desire to continue my education. But now that I had had a taste of the business world, with all of its fulfillment and fame, I changed my mind. Surprisingly, my parents took the news well and supported me in the decision. Time, that great healer, had put distance between what I had done to Grandma back when the company was in the garage, and who I was now. As far as my parents knew, I was a legitimate businessman, making it against all odds. They believed the stories they read in the newspapers about their son, the entrepreneur. And, by keeping them unaware of my illegal activities, I gave them no reason to doubt what they believed.

As I turned eighteen, my family, friends, the business community, and the media all saw me as one of the top ten entrepreneurs of the 1980s. I had done a great job of concealing how I had achieved my success. No one knew who I really was.

Each year that passed became a measure of my performance with ZZZZ Best. If, at eighteen, I had not achieved greater financial gain than I did at seventeen, I considered myself a failure. And the trauma didn't stop there: I became paranoid about my media worth. Each year I aged, so too did "The Barry Minkow Story."

My story was unique not because I was a businessman, but because I was an *eighteen-year-old entrepreneur who had started his company at age sixteen*. My youth had been the key, but now that youth was giving way to adulthood, I had to ponder the ominous question: How long could I continue to hold the public's attention? The thought of losing recognition gripped me in a way I'll not soon forget. The only way to remain *big* in the eyes of society was to grow and expand each year. If I could increase the number of offices and employees and expand ZZZZ Best's geographic coverage, I would be able to overcome the age factor and stay in the spotlight.

This added pressure dramatically changed my philosophy about doing business. I would have strong guilt feelings, not for the crimes I had committed, but for failing to be the first to arrive at the office and the last to leave. Consequently, I put unrealistic demands on myself and evolved into an intolerant, impatient perfectionist who was never satisfied. Even on weekends I couldn't rest. If by accident I slept in one day, I'd have to explain to my family and friends how hard I had worked all week, to justify some much-needed rest. I wasn't satisfied unless people viewed me as the hardest and most dedicated worker they'd ever seen.

❖ ❖ ❖

With only ninety days of high school left, I tried to "tread water" financially until I could dedicate my full attention to the company. Although spring is usually the best time of year for the carpet-cleaning industry, production in both offices was down. And because I was totally dependent on the day-to-day sales to pay the bills, I was in trouble. As always. The cash demands of a company with fifty employees grew so onerous that I waited until after 6:00 P.M. on Fridays to pass out payroll checks, knowing that with the banks closed, they couldn't be cashed. This really upset the employees, many of whom saw through this tactic and threatened to quit. One week several of my carpet cleaners tried to cash their checks early Monday morning while I was at school. With no money in the account, Town Bank turned them away. Just weeks from being able to devote my full attention to the company, I was in danger of losing it. But I'd been in similar predicaments before and knew what I had to do.

To resolve this latest crisis, I exercised my newly acquired legal rights—I was finally eighteen—by opening a checking account at five different banks! I then took a few of the temporary checks from my new accounts and deposited over seven thousand dollars into my Town Bank account. Having gained the confidence of Doug Fitzgerald and others at the bank, I got immediate credit on the checks. This helped me to cover the payroll and avoid a massive walkout. But to avoid detection, I had to cover the temporary checks.

To do this, I staged a break-in at the Thousand Oaks office. This time, however, the adjuster for my new insurance carrier— the other company had canceled my policy after the first claim— said it would take a week before the draft would be ready. After I promised to pay him a thousand dollars interest plus the principal within a week, Jerry Williams lent me more money. I had pulled off another check-kiting scheme. I received the draft for almost seventeen thousand dollars six days later—just in time to cover the next payroll.

Rumors spread within the company that I had staged the Thousand Oaks break-in. Many felt two burglaries in six months was impossible, or at least highly suspicious. I met this problem head-on by requiring all employees to attend a company meeting. I spoke boldly and blamed the break-ins on "jealous competition." "If you owned a carpet-cleaning company and some eighteen-year-old kid came along and stole a lot of your business, would you just sit around, or would you try to bury him?" They believed me and the rumors stopped. Another fire had been put out.

❖ ❖ ❖

As my senior year came to a close, I was satisfied that I had accomplished every goal I had set for myself during that memorable basketball game in tenth grade. Like most high schools, Cleveland had contests for "Most Popular," "Most Likely to Succeed," and many others. I was one of the few students who won two awards: "Most Likely to Succeed" and "Class Clown." In my eyes, this proved that ZZZZ Best had met my deepest need—acceptance!

After graduation ceremonies, my class celebrated at Magic Mountain. I took one of my very attractive employees—one of the perks of signing the paychecks. The hundreds of classmates partying and having a good time that evening knew nothing of the real world and didn't have a clue about how to run a business. They were just a bunch of kids compared to me. I happily separated myself from these immature high school graduates who had no desire for fame and fortune. *I have accomplished more in two years than most of these guys will achieve in their entire lives,* I thought.

On the way home that evening, I put my arm around my tired girlfriend and thought about what I had missed during high school. ZZZZ Best had prevented me from attending many football games, parties, and social gatherings. But that had been my choice. I had willingly given up high school "fun" for big-time "finance." My date fell asleep and, as I sped down the quiet freeway that warm summer night, I knew my educational career had ended. I resolved to make an impact on the business world that no one would ever forget.

No *wonder I'm always short of cash,* I said to myself. *These guys are stealing from me!* I soon realized that people had taken advantage of my high school distractions. Some of the carpet cleaners were arriving at their scheduled appointments, suggesting that the customers call the company and cancel the job, and then cleaning the carpets for much less money—which they pocketed. I had lost a significant amount of business and fired one of the men involved. Out of school for only a few weeks, I was already seeing the benefits of "hands-on management."

Next I promoted Mike McGee to be my "right-hand man." A dedicated, hard worker who gave ZZZZ Best 100 percent every day, Mike had been with me since the garage days and had earned my total trust. He looked up to me and, because I feared losing his respect, I didn't tell him of my past or present crimes. Together we attempted to straighten out the company's many problems.

As the money from the Thousand Oaks "burglary" dwindled away, I considered new means of raising funds. I was tired of waiting until the last minute and then panicking to cover payroll. I wanted to stay ahead of the financial game. Two things helped me do this. First, I put a "Money Wanted" ad in the *L. A. Times,* hoping to find a willing investor. Second, I met a man named Paul Weaver.

Paul owned a construction company. Like Jerry Williams, he

was very wealthy and often invested in other businesses. Though he was much older than I, we got along well and he had become interested in ZZZZ Best. He was impressed by the fact that I ran my own business at such a young age.

One summer day in 1984, after Paul and I had finished working out at the health club, he came to visit my Reseda branch. After a quick tour of the facility (by then I had leased additional office space), we retired to my office.

"So, how much would it cost me to get in on the action, Barry?"

His question caught me off guard. I wasn't used to people asking to give me money. "I don't know, Paul. What would you feel comfortable with?"

"Listen, kid," he said sternly, "I'm a businessman. When I see a deal I like, I go for it." He paused. "I like what you've got going here and I want in. You tell me how much you want."

The good news was that he wasn't looking for a "partner-ship" or a percentage of the company. I would retain 100 percent control over ZZZZ Best, regardless. The bad news was that his money was going to be expensive. But I was used to that.

"Well, I'm thinking of opening another office in Anaheim," I said. "But it's going to be pretty expensive. Can you afford twenty-five thousand?"

He didn't even blink. "Tomorrow I want you to go to my bank and pick up a twenty-five-thousand-dollar cashier's check." He got up from the chair and walked toward the door. "Every Monday, I'll expect you to give me twelve hundred *in cash*—seven hundred to reduce the principal and five hundred interest. Can you afford those payments?"

I smiled. That was much more money than Jerry had ever lent me. *Should I have asked for more?* "You bet I can. Anaheim is the perfect place for a new location. I'll 'clean up' over there."

"Write down my beeper number. If you ever need me for any reason, just call and I'll get back to you."

I wrote down his number, went over to shake his hand, and he strode off.

With all the internal problems and financial difficulties, I didn't think opening more locations was possible or wise. But because I needed to give Paul a legitimate reason for his loan, I was forced to expand before the company was ready. As I sat in my office, I thought about how angry Jerry would be if he knew about my new relationship with Paul. For that reason, I told Jerry nothing about him.

A few days later, Rick Price, an investor in the Los Angeles area, responded to my ad in the *L. A. Times*. To stay ahead of any future cash-flow crunch, I agreed to meet with him.

After touring our offices, Mr. Price asked me some technical questions about the company's gross sales, net profit per store, and related financial conditions. Basically, he wanted financial statements. Unlike Paul and Jerry, who were streetsmart and knew how to hustle, Mr. Price was a professional who had made millions over the years.

To impress him (and to get some of his money), I needed someone who could prepare financial statements for ZZZZ Best. Through an acquaintance I found a public accountant who asked to see all my company records. Unfortunately, my records were in such poor shape he found it impossible to track my past business activity. But if I didn't have a profit-and-loss statement that confirmed the company's earnings, Mr. Price wouldn't lend me any money.

So I convinced the accountant, for a large fee, to prepare bogus financial statements and tax returns confirming large profits, which didn't exist. Although Rick Price preferred CPA-prepared statements, he accepted the statements prepared by my public accountant and agreed to loan me thirty thousand dollars. Interestingly, his payment schedule was identical to Paul's: a weekly amount of about twelve hundred, with seven hundred to pay down the principal and the balance as interest, cleverly disguised as an "advisor's fee." Mr. Price also had me sign an agreement—something Paul and Jerry had never done—that forced me to pledge my company as collateral.

I was amazed how a man of Mr. Price's caliber would set up a loan requiring such high interest. But if he chose to be blinded by greed, I had no problem taking advantage of him. Or was he taking advantage of me?

My relationship with Doug Fitzgerald and Town Bank continued to improve. Doug allowed me to open a merchant account that enabled ZZZZ Best to accept MasterCard and Visa, making sales easier. He even eased up on monitoring my account, which allowed me to slip the large deposits from Paul Weaver and Rick Price in without incident. With this unprecedented cash surplus, I decided to start playing the part of the "big-time businessman." Until mid-1984, I had spent most of the ZZZZ Best proceeds on company expansion and paying people off. I still lived at home and drove an older car. I needed tangible personal assets to prove that ZZZZ Best was really "making it."

So I went to Granada Nissan and purchased a brand-new, twenty-thousand-dollar 300ZX. To build my credit, I bought the car on time, putting only six thousand down. Because 1984 was the first year for the 300ZX, many people stared as I drove down the highway. The car became my eloquent rebuttal to skeptics who doubted that ZZZZ Best was earning "big bucks." Then I purchased a brand-new, two-bedroom condominium in Canoga Park, one with a view of the pool. Although I couldn't move in until March of 1985, I was satisfied, since I had something significant to show for two years as a businessman.

The new car improved my social life considerably. Girls who had never given me a second glance were now anxious to go out with an entrepreneur in his flashy sports car. Magazines, newspapers, and local television shows also boosted my image with more tales of the "Amazing Barry Minkow Story." To make up for the time I had lost in high school, I took advantage of the situation by dating as many women as possible. And then Donna Hill came into my life.

In September of 1984, my sister Sheri was hospitalized for several months. Donna was at the same hospital. I visited the hospital every day—partly to see Sheri and partly to get to know Donna. She was a very attractive sixteen-year-old blonde who even looked great without makeup. To impress her, I went out of my way to tell her about ZZZZ Best, my new car, and the condo. I even showed her newspaper articles about myself. And to cover all the bases, I showed up in a tank top and shorts, hoping that if my money and material possessions didn't impress her, perhaps my body would. It worked. Donna was interested in me, and during her stay in the hospital we got to know each other better.

❖   ❖   ❖

Mike had tried to tell me that opening the Anaheim office would be a mistake; we didn't have the management depth to handle another location. But because I wanted it, he was determined to make it work. I relocated several key people from the two existing offices, hoping they could run Anaheim profitably. Not only did the Anaheim office lose money, however, but the other locations suffered as well from the removal of their key people. Now I was stuck with three unprofitable stores and the large weekly loan payments.

To make things worse, one of my employees went to work for another carpet-cleaning company and spread word that I was losing "big money" and was in danger of "going under." The rumor made the rounds of the competition and got back to all the ZZZZ Best offices.

As I fought to keep up company morale, a manager from one of my biggest competitors thought it would be fun to steal some of my employees right out from under my nose. I showed up at the Reseda office just as he was assuring two of my men that I was going out of business. Rather than make a scene, I asked him to step into my office. Once the door was closed, I asked where he got off coming to my office trying to steal my people.

"You're going down, Barry!" he shouted. "Everybody knows it. So why don't you let some of your good people get hooked up with a stable company before the fall?"

"What makes you so sure I'm going out of business?" I asked, trying to stay calm.

"Your own people are saying it! Anaheim's a loser and it's made the whole company a loser—"

It took everything I had not to jump across the desk and start beating on the guy. He knew nothing about what I had been through—to keep the company going and to avoid failure. I stormed around the desk and shook my finger in his face. "Let me tell you something, pal! Don't you ever let me catch you at any of my offices, trying to steal my people! And you can go back and tell your boss and everybody else that ZZZZ Best will *never* go down! You got that?"

He watched me closely, seeing the sincerity in my eyes, before turning toward the door.

"You're in the big leagues now, where nothing lasts forever . . . not even ZZZZ Best" was his parting shot.

"Oh, yeah?" I growled. "Just try to stop me. If you or anybody else tries to get in my way, I'll run you over! Count on it!"

❖   ❖   ❖

Maybe the pressure is getting to me, I thought to myself as I drove to visit Donna and Sheri at the hospital. The responsibilities of one hundred employees and three offices and the pressures from the competition and the various investors had stripped words like *peace* and *contentment* of their meaning. My onetime cash surplus had dwindled to under ten thousand dollars—far short of what I needed to pay the weekly bills. Yet again I faced a financial crisis that could crush me—unless I thought of another way to raise capital.

On the passenger seat of my 300ZX lay the daily deposits for the Reseda office. Because of my unexpected visitor, I hadn't gotten to the bank in time to deposit them. Pausing at a stoplight, I looked over the two stacks of deposit slips—one for customers who paid by check and the other for customers who paid by credit card—and realized that the credit card slips were written in *by hand,* not imprinted. With so many crews in the field, it would have been impossible to give each an imprinter. As long as the customer signed the credit card slip, the bank agreed to accept the deposit.

If I used the names and numbers of my legitimate credit card customers to make up additional slips in large amounts and forged their signatures, I could raise immediate cash. Of course, the customers would dispute the charges, but that would take months. In the meantime, I'd have free use of their money. By the time I pulled into the hospital parking lot, I had it all planned: The following morning I would start creating bogus credit card slips.

❖ ❖ ❖

Jerry had asked to meet with me privately a week earlier, but because I was otherwise occupied—writing phony credit card receipts—I had been able to put him off until now.

"I'm not an idiot, Barry," he groused. "I see this Rick Price guy and Paul coming around the office. I know you're probably getting money from them . . . and I don't care." He waited for me to look up from my telephone messages. "I only care about *me!* You'd have nothing if I hadn't helped you get started."

"I know that, and I appreciate what you've done for me. You're my friend for life," I said, and returned to my work.

"Good, I'm glad you feel that way, because I want you to do something for me." I stopped everything and listened. "I see your new car and I want the same thing."

So, this was Jerry's price for my freedom. It was futile to argue with him. He was still a little stronger, a little meaner, and a whole lot more experienced than I. If I complied with the monthly car payments, I would be free to borrow and deal with whomever I wanted, without looking over my shoulder to see if he was watching. To me, that was worth *two* cars.

Jerry had loaned me money off and on in ZZZZ Best's early history. We'd never kept an accurate accounting, what with the heavy interest payments, so it wasn't clear what the principal balance was at any given time. We just mutually assumed I had a limitless obligation to him for making ZZZZ Best possible.

"No problem," I said calmly. I reached across the desk and shook his hand. "Let me know who to send the car payments to."

Jerry was satisfied. He had gotten exactly what he wanted. As for me, I concluded that some battles weren't worth fighting. I knew there would come a time when I would be released from the clutches of Jerry Williams, and I looked forward to that day.

With my cash demands temporarily eased by the credit card fraud, Mike and I determined to spend more time, from November 1984 to February 1985, shoring up the Thousand Oaks and Anaheim offices. At least twice weekly, I drove to Anaheim. I enjoyed spending time in my car, away from the pressures of ZZZZ Best. I also enjoyed passing a building, visible from the southbound lanes of the Santa Ana Freeway, upon which a big sign spelled out inspirational sayings like "Tough Times Never Last, But Tough People Do." I looked forward to reading what the sign said whenever I went to Anaheim. It was as if I were thirsty for spiritual information but unwilling to search beyond what casually or accidentally crossed my path during my busy life.

❖   ❖   ❖

After Donna and Sheri were released from the hospital late in 1984, every night after work I drove to Donna's home to spend time with her. Convinced that money could buy everything, I bought her a car, jewelry, clothes—anything she wanted. She was the first girl I had ever loved. She was beautiful, very loyal to me, and wanted to make me happy. I had thought that would be enough to satisfy me. But I was wrong. Something was still missing. Although I couldn't put my finger on just what it was, I attempted to fill this void by dating other women behind her back.

❖   ❖   ❖

By February 1985, Mike and I had jacked up the company's productivity. Whether the locations actually made money, it was impossible to tell, because of the heavy loans and other expenses they were forced to absorb. Nevertheless, gross sales were substantially higher—an important point for those of us who lived week to week.

When I went to Town Bank to paint Doug Fitzgerald a brighter picture than usual, I learned that the bank had fallen on hard times and been forced by the FDIC to close its doors. Doug was moving to another bank—Third Union, and I immediately moved the company accounts along with him. Despite Doug's efforts, it took almost three weeks before I could open another merchant account and begin depositing more credit card slips. The delay nearly buried me. Once opened, I made up for lost time by running almost one thousand dollars worth of phony drafts through the account daily. It wasn't long before they were on to me.

A disturbed and disappointed Doug Fitzgerald summoned me to his office one spring morning. He told me the bank had discovered that I had processed close to fifty thousand dollars worth of bogus credit-card charges. To protect themselves, they had frozen the ZZZZ Best accounts and bounced all my checks. Doug was powerless to help.

Faced with the possibility of losing everything, I asked Paul for a $30,000 loan. Based on my consistent payments on the first loan, he willingly gave me the money. Then I borrowed $12,500 from Jerry, promising to have it back to him in two months—with interest. Finally, I went to Rick Price. For months he and I had talked about a $45,000 loan and, because I was in trouble, I took his money as well. Within a two-week period, I raised over $80,000—enough to cover the bad checks and get a fresh start at a new bank, National Federal Savings and Loan. Doug agreed to give me a good recommendation if I promised (in writing) to pay back the credit card vouchers as they came in. I even put $10,000 in Third Union Bank as a gesture of good faith.

Even though Doug briefly interrogated me on the credit card incident—I blamed the fraud on "unscrupulous subcontractors"—it seemed the banks were more interested in recovering their losses than in prosecuting any wrongdoing. There were no legal repercussions. This made a lasting impression on me. As long as I paid the money back and nobody got hurt, I could do whatever I wanted. And I did.

❖ ❖ ❖

To celebrate my nineteenth birthday, *Entrepreneur* magazine profiled me as the "Entrepreneur of the Month" for March of 1985. The publicity couldn't have come at a more opportune time. The credit-card fraud had tainted my credibility with some in the financial community and with ZZZZ Best telephone personnel who took customers' complaints about overcharges. I used the entrepreneur "title" to corroborate the authenticity of ZZZZ

Best, then made sure all the employees read the article and even sent a copy to Warner Center Bank, hoping to earn their trust.

Also in March, I moved into the Canoga Park condominium, having furnished it for under ten thousand dollars. Leaving home was tough, but it was time for Barry Minkow the businessman to take advantage of his success. I brought over Mom, Vera, and Mike—the three employees who had been with me since the garage days—and they checked the place out, admiring my success. They each possessed the one quality that I demanded above all else: 100 percent devotion and loyalty to me, at all times.

The excitement generated by the *Entrepreneur* magazine award, coupled with the purchase of the condo, helped ease the pain of turning nineteen. Though I was getting older, my accomplishments (as far as anyone knew) were keeping pace with my age. I was still newsworthy and was determined to continue to be, no matter what it took.

❖ ❖ ❖

My March celebration soon came to a sobering halt. The credit card drafts bombarded me in April, wiping out my ten-thousand-dollar cushion and causing Doug to call me daily. Fearing prosecution if I didn't pay, I delivered funds to Third Union Bank twice weekly. I also had to come up with the weekly loan payments to Paul, Jerry, and Rick Price. Company payrolls and expenses reached an all-time high. And large yellow-pages ads, purchased in several phone books back when I thought the credit card fraud would last forever, were now coming due—to the tune of almost five thousand dollars per month!

My larger problem was that of limited options. With my three investors "maxed out," I had nowhere to replenish my cash position. There was no way the three offices could support all the expenses. Plus, I had promised to open a San Diego office soon. Several of my key cleaners and solicitors had their hearts set on relocating to ZZZZ Best's newest branch. If I didn't follow through, I would have a serious morale problem on my hands.

By the end of April, I was back to kiting checks, buying time until I could come up with a temporary cure for my financial ills. I fell behind in payments to Rick Price and was surprised when he cut me no slack and tried to foreclose against the company, assuming that repossessing my equipment would shut me down.

When the marshals handed me a subpoena to appear in court, I immediately went to a lawyer for advice. After reading the agreements, he told me that if the judge ruled against me, ZZZZ Best would be out of business. But for some reason, I wasn't scared. I had been through similar situations and had always come out on top. I was confident that once again I would figure out some way to solve the problem.

We went to court and our defense was the truth; namely, that Mr. Price was charging me an illegal rate of interest on the loan. The judge believed us. In fact, he called Mr. Price a usurer, stating that he had no experience in the carpet-cleaning industry and was therefore undeserving of his "advisory fees." I had dodged another bullet. The ruling forced Rick Price to accept monthly payments on a significantly reduced principal balance.

Even with this victory, as May came to a close, I was in deep financial trouble. My checks began to bounce, and it looked as if my luck had run out. As I was sitting in my office, trying desperately to figure out some way to hold things together, the phone rang. Although I didn't know it then, the second I picked up the receiver, my life was to change—forever.

A New Source of Cash | 8

"Hi, Ralph, how are you?" I asked as I tried to focus on his call.

"I'm good, Barry. How's business?"

"Good . . . good," I lied. "How can I help you?"

"I've got a very special carpet-repair job for you. It's in a town house development. The guy has a busted seam and needs a cleaning."

"No problem, Ralph. I'll have a crew over there tomorrow."

"Okay. But I need *you* to do the job personally. The customer is refusing to close escrow unless it's done right." There was a short silence. "He's supposed to be a mob-type guy, Barry. His name is Ron Knox. . . . He's very wealthy and very dangerous."

Although I hadn't heard of Ron Knox, I'd heard the mob often lent money to small businesses. Ralph had my interest. "When do you want this job done?"

"Today, if possible. Are you busy right now?"

"Yeah, but I can swing by there—"

"Listen, Barry," he interrupted me, "I want you to be careful with this guy. He's got a reputation."

I shrugged off his concern. "Don't worry, Ralph. I'll be fine."

I got the address, picked up the keys to one of the trucks, and was on my way. I had seen movies and television shows that portrayed gangsters as loan sharks who "bust up people who don't pay." But I was desperate the day I pulled into Ron Knox's driveway, and I was willing to do business with anyone—even if it meant pledging my life as collateral.

❖　❖　❖

"So, you're the whiz kid I keep reading about." Ron Knox was about fifty years old, and impeccably dressed. From his seat at the dining room table, he was watching me glue together a seam in his hallway carpet. "I saved that February article in the *Herald-Examiner* that profiled your company. The press really seems to like you."

I smiled and kept working. "It's good for business, Mr. Knox," I said. "And I never turn them down."

"Neither did I when I ran my own company," he bragged.

"Really?" I looked up from my work, pretending an interest in his past business dealings.

"Yeah. I started a company out of my house. After years of hard work, we went public and the stock was worth millions."

I didn't know much about stock and public companies, but I didn't want to let Ron know that. "What happened?" I asked curiously.

Ron got up out of his chair, walked to the kitchen counter and picked up several articles. He brought them to where I was working and dropped them at my side.

"The government took everything from me because they said I didn't follow the rules. Once they put a 'jacket' like that on you, it's only a matter of time before you fail." I glanced at the articles. Ron Knox and his company had been front-page news at one time. "But originally I started out like you did. In fact, we've got more in common than you think."

I removed the steaming iron, set it on its stand, and walked over to the dining-room table. This was the opportunity I'd been waiting for. "I just bet we do," I said, smiling. "Did you have trouble raising money and getting bank loans?"

Ron Knox moved and answered questions slowly and thoughtfully. He was in no hurry and kept things under control. "Sure I did. But I had some close associates who lent me money when I needed it. How about you?"

I took a deep breath and forced myself to look distraught. "I'm not that lucky, Mr. Knox. I've got three stores, almost one hundred employees, and could grow even bigger if I had the capital. But for some reason, no one wants to lend a nineteen-year-old businessman any money."

Ron listened attentively. "How much money will you need to expand?"

I thought back to my first meeting with Paul, when I had given him a low figure in answer to the same question. I wouldn't make that mistake again. "About one hundred thousand dollars."

"It costs that much to open a few rug-cleaning stores?" Ron asked a bit skeptically.

He probably wanted to hear a specific use for the money. Knowing I couldn't lie about the cost of opening a carpet-cleaning location, I remembered the time I had deposited a large insurance draft into my Town Bank account and told Doug it was for work done on a restoration job.

"No, it doesn't," I replied honestly. "But the company performs restoration services on buildings damaged by fire and water. And the bigger the job, the more money I need to buy materials and supplies to complete it."

Ron listened carefully to my every word. "How many of these jobs do you have going right now?"

"Three," I lied. "One in Torrance, one in South Pasadena, and the other in San Diego. That's where my next office is going—*if* I can raise the money."

Ron pushed a few newspapers around on the table and picked up a pad and pen. After jotting a few notes to himself, he opened his briefcase and pulled out the February 1985 *Herald-Examiner* article.

"So you're the big Barry Minkow." His laughter eased the tension. "I'll tell you what I'll do for you, kid." He scribbled an address on his notepad and handed it to me. "Later on today, I want you to stop by my office. Bring me your financial statements and some proof of these insurance-restoration jobs, and I'll raise you all the money you'll ever need."

With great difficulty I restrained my enthusiasm. It had taken less than thirty minutes for Ron Knox to solve a problem that had hampered me for two and a half years. "I'm just about done here, so if you'll give me until four o'clock, I think I can get you everything you asked for."

He nodded with satisfaction. "Four o'clock it is. I'll look forward to it."

❖ ❖ ❖

On the way back from Ron's town house, I thought about the items he had requested. The financial statements were no problem; my accountant had prepared those for the Rick Price deal. But how would I prove I had thousands of dollars in restoration business? And what would happen to me if Ron Knox lent me the money and found out I was lying about the jobs?

Unfortunately, I had no other choice. I suppressed the "Mob-Busts-Up-White-Kid" headlines that passed through my mind and focused on what I needed to get done to keep the company running. As long as Ron got his money back, nothing would ever happen to me—I hoped.

❖ ❖ ❖

"This is Gary Todd," said the person on the other end of the line.

"Hi, Gary, it's Barry. How's it going?"

"Good, partner. How's business?" he asked fondly.

"Great! Is Partner Insurance keeping you busy?"

Gary had left Trust Insurance for Partner, mostly because of me. In 1983 I had abused our friendship by falsifying two Trust drafts. Gary hadn't been fired, but his superiors had questioned why he had entrusted claims to a seventeen-year-old kid. He resigned and was later hired by Partner Insurance.

"Yeah, I'm busy. But it keeps me out of trouble. What's on your mind?"

"Do you feel like making twenty-five hundred dollars for doing nothing?"

"Depends on what kind of 'nothing.'"

"Well, Gary, I'm going to level with you. I've got a guy who will lend me all the money I'll ever want—if I can confirm to him that I'm doing large restoration jobs. What I need are a few letterheads from Partner's and for you to confirm three or four jobs. To play it safe, I'll put your *direct* number on the letter so that when people call, they'll only reach you." I gave Gary a chance to think about what I had said before I continued. "If it wasn't a life-or-death situation, I wouldn't ask you this, Gary. But I'm hurting real bad, and I've got a hundred employees depending on me."

"All right," he said in a soft tone. "Come by and pick up the letterhead."

❖   ❖   ❖

Amy, my secretary, trusted me. If I told her to type out contract verifications on Partner letterhead, she assumed it was for a legitimate purpose. Amy was an organizer, a hard worker, and someone who cared for me as if I were her own son.

With my financial statements, three phony restoration work orders totaling almost $250,000, and the verification letter supposedly signed by Gary Todd in hand, I made my way to Ron's large, elegant office building. Before I went in, I contemplated whether or not I should go through with the plan. Would Ron Knox really harm me if he found out about my con? Was ZZZZ Best worth risking my well-being? I answered these questions with a turn of the doorknob.

An attractive secretary greeted me. "Yes, Mr. Minkow, Ron and Dean are expecting you. Just go right in," she said, pointing to the door opposite her.

"Well, I see you made it on time," said Ron when I stepped into the room. "Barry Minkow, I'd like you to meet Dean De-Witt."

We shook hands, and I sat next to Ron, while DeWitt seated himself at the desk.

"Did you bring the documents?" Ron asked.

"Sure did." I handed him the folder and he began to examine its contents.

"So how long has ZZZZ Best been in business?" Dean asked.

"I started the company at age sixteen, in October of 1982. That's when the DBA was officially recorded. A few months ago my attorney advised me to form a private corporation, and I did."

"Are you the sole owner of all the corporation's stock?" Ron interjected.

"I am."

"Why don't you just go to a bank and get a loan for your business?" Dean asked.

Already I didn't like this guy. But if I was going to save ZZZZ Best, I needed to answer his questions. "Banks and I have never gotten along," I admitted. "When I opened the company, several of them closed my accounts because I was underage. When I turned eighteen and tried to get a loan, they explained that I needed a three-year track record plus hard assets to pledge as security."

Ron passed some of the documents to Dean, and they read in silence.

Eventually Dean looked up. "If we call this Gary Todd guy at Partner, will he verify these contracts?"

"Yes, he will." My heart beat faster.

Ron motioned to Dean, who left the room with his letter from Partner, then turned to me. "How much will you make on these contracts?"

I had to think of a figure. "About eighty thousand dollars in profit when all is said and done."

Ron nodded and looked back at the financial statements. "Assuming everything checks out, I'll raise the money for these projects from a few friends of mine, and we can split the profit on the jobs. Does that sound fair?"

"Sure does," I replied brightly. In reality, I was desperate; I had bad checks to cover. "The problem is, I have to purchase some materials immediately or I could lose one of these contracts. How long will this whole process take?"

Ron smiled. "I just met you, kid. Slow down—I'll take care of everything."

Just then Dean DeWitt came back. "It checks out," he told Ron. I breathed easier. Gary had come through again.

"We need to fix these financial statements," Ron said.

"No problem," Dean answered. "I'll get Carl Stowe on it right away."

"Good. And then we'll take him to some banks and see if we can't arrange a line of credit," Ron said.

I was concerned. Bank loans take a long time, and that was one thing I didn't have. "I appreciate the effort, but I don't think *any* bank will lend me money. And I've got jobs to complete now!"

The two men looked at each other and smiled.

"Never let it be said that I stopped progress," Ron replied. "Come by my house tomorrow and pick up ten thousand dollars. That should get you started. Then I'll meet you here late next week and have one of my associates give you another twenty-five.

That will buy us enough time to arrange a bank loan or, if that doesn't work, to raise some money from Lee Herring."

"Who?"

"He's a close friend. I'm supposed to be broke, so I've got to finance my business ventures through friends. But you don't need to worry about that. Just get these jobs done and run that company. I'll take care of the rest."

After a few questions, I got up to leave. But then I remembered the agreements Rick Price had asked me to sign before giving me any money. "Will you be wanting me to sign any loan documents, Mr. Knox?"

"For now, that won't be necessary, kid. Just pay me back and everything will go smoothly. . . . I trust you, Barry. And I'm helping you because you remind me of myself when I started out."

❖   ❖   ❖

I covered most of the bad checks with the ten thousand dollars. While I was waiting for the twenty-five thousand, Ron Knox visited the office. I introduced him as a friend doing business with the company.

Mike and Amy came to me immediately after he left; Ron worried them, they had heard he was reported to have crime connections. I downplayed our relationship, assuring them that I was in complete control of ZZZZ Best. Yet, deep down I knew that was no longer true.

Dealing with Ron Knox inspired me to work out more regularly. Although I'd never decreased my steroid use, the stress of running ZZZZ Best had forced me to miss many workouts. Ron scared me, and that got me into the gym. He drove a large, black Cadillac—the kind driven by the "bad guys" on television. He called me often and had his finger on the pulse of my daily activities. I wasn't naive enough to believe that muscles would stop bullets, but a consistent workout program did give me more confidence in dealing with the new realities of my business life.

❖ ❖ ❖

Late Friday afternoon I walked into Ron's office building. Traffic on the highway was heavy as people rushed home to begin the weekend. No one seemed to notice or care that I was about to "sell my soul to the devil."

The secretary was answering phones as I entered the office. She motioned for me to go right in. I found Ron Knox by himself.

"Hi, kid! How's business?" he asked.

I felt like telling him the truth: If I didn't get the twenty-five thousand, all one hundred of the payroll checks I'd just issued would bounce. But I hoped I sounded believable when I said, "Business is good. We're anxious to get those restoration projects started."

"I want you to take a look at these." Ron handed me financial statements and tax returns for ZZZZ Best for 1983 and 1984.

The documents were much more detailed than my accountant's had been—professionally prepared, with footnotes. They also showed higher earnings and an inflated balance sheet. I was happy—no, proud—to be president of the company represented by these statements.

"What do you think?" Ron asked.

"They look great. No bank will turn me down for a loan now. Who did these?"

He paused before answering. "Carl Stowe. He owns some retail shops and has an accounting business on the side."

Just then the intercom buzzed. It was the receptionist. "Donald is here to see you, Ron."

"Send him in."

The second I saw Donald Snyder, I stopped perusing my new financial statements. He had dark hair pulled back into a short ponytail, a mean look on his face, and he filled the door frame. He was carrying a paper sack.

"Donald Snyder, meet Barry Minkow," Ron introduced us.

I rose from my chair and went over to shake his hand.

"I read about you in the papers," Donald said brusquely.

I smiled nervously and nodded. Donald was an intimidating man.

"Does the kid know the rules?"

"Since it's your money, I thought I'd leave that to you," Ron said, smiling.

Donald tossed me the brown bag. "You pay every Tuesday. I don't care how long you keep the money as long as you pay every week. You got that, pal?"

I got it. The same deal as with Paul and Jerry, only Donald came on ten times stronger. "No problem. I can handle that. Should I give the money to Ron every week?"

Donald looked at Ron. Ron nodded. "Yeah, just give it to him," Donald agreed.

I couldn't resist the temptation to peek into the sack.

"It's all there, kid. You don't have to count it. Twenty-five thousand dollars! Listen, Ron, I've got to go downtown, so unless there's anything else, I'll call you later."

"That'll be fine, Donald. I'll be home most of the night."

Before he left, Donald wanted to tell me one more thing. "Look, kid, I don't know you. The only reason you're getting this money is because of Ron. But if you miss payments or try to beat me for the money, you'll have problems—big problems."

He didn't need to threaten me—but it worked anyway. I was scared. "You won't have any problems with me, Mr. Snyder," I replied.

He stared at me for a second, smiled enigmatically, lightly patted me on the cheek—just like in the movies—and was gone.

"Before you leave," Ron began, "I want you to sign these tax returns so we can submit them to a few banks."

I promptly obeyed. If I could say at the end of any given day that the only illegal thing I had done was sign a few fake tax returns, I was doing well.

"Also, I want to rent a small office near yours. My family has a candy distribution company, and we need a location to store inventory and take incoming orders. I can't think of anywhere else I'd rather be than near you," he said chummily.

The last thing I wanted was Ron Knox and his "associates" hanging around my main office. People would think criminals had taken over my business. But I was in too deep to say no. Also, I needed the bank loans he was about to arrange.

As I turned to walk away, I realized that I didn't know what my weekly payment was on Donald's loan. "By the way, Ron, how much do I give you every week for this money?"

"Five points a week, kid—that's the going rate."

"How much is that in dollars and cents?"

"Twelve hundred and fifty dollars a week—interest only," he said sternly.

I should have known.

❖ ❖ ❖

"Barry Minkow, I'd like you to meet Lee Herring and Julie Kennedy," said Ron Knox as I entered Lee's home. Ron had set up the meeting in hopes of raising one hundred thousand dollars from Lee and a few of his friends.

"Did you bring the documentation with you?" he asked. Ron wanted Lee and Julie to see the phony financial statements, the letter from Gary confirming the three restoration jobs, and the work orders substantiating their dollar amounts. I handed him a neatly assembled file folder.

Lee was a nice man who, according to Ron, loved pursuing this type of financial adventure. Julie was extremely attractive and a good listener. She had just been through some rough times and was looking to improve her cash situation. Both were said to be wealthy and anxious to invest. In fact, Ron had made it clear that if I could impress Lee, I could raise endless amounts of money because of his many contacts.

Ron did most of the talking; I simply sat back and answered questions. The investors were told that ZZZZ Best needed approximately one hundred thousand dollars to complete the three projects. The offer was simple: The two could each invest up to one hundred thousand, and in return would receive 2 percent a week (in cash) as interest on their money, until the principal balance was paid off.

"How can you afford to pay us that much on our money, Barry?" Lee asked.

"The profit margin on these jobs averages 30 to 35 percent. If we're doing two-hundred-fifty-thousand-dollars worth of restoration work, the company will net over eighty thousand for three months' work. So, the cost of the money is absorbed in the large profits." I was getting good at this. I knew all the right words and could even look people right in the eye and lie to them. By the time I left Lee's house, I knew the loan was a done deal.

❖　❖　❖

Donna had asked that we go to the Renaissance Fair in Agoura Hills because I hadn't been spending enough quality time with her. She was right. That Sunday afternoon we held hands and toured the crowded fairgrounds. Hundreds of people milled about, enjoying the exhibits featuring the art, food, and culture that had made the Renaissance such a significant time in world history. But I wasn't one of them. For me, the fair was merely a comma in my business life—a life that now involved a connection to the underworld.

Still, I was uneasy and I watched the young children running from display to display, without a care in the world. *Donald Snyder and Ron Knox aren't looking over their shoulders,* I thought.

At seventeen, Donna was getting prettier all the time. I loved being with her, but though I had introduced her to Ron, she had no idea of the extent of my involvement with him. She assumed I was a legitimate businessman—the boy genius the newspapers kept writing about. I felt all alone. Despite being surrounded by hundreds of families, I had no one I could talk to about my problems. After all, who would ever believe me? I worried that I might be bringing Donna down with me. Would someone hurt her if I didn't pay? I forced the thought from my mind.

❖   ❖   ❖

Lee, Julie, and one other person made up the first investment group. The large influx of cash allowed me to pay Paul off completely, catch Jerry up, pay the company's outstanding debts, and open my fourth office in San Diego. Mike and I had learned the secret to opening a successful office. We introduced our company with a large direct mailing to thousands of homes, then followed up with telephone soliciting. This helped us generate large amounts of business and start off profitably.

Despite the success in San Diego and a cash position that allowed me to stop kiting checks, there were still major problems at ZZZZ Best. By early August, rumors had spread throughout the industry that ZZZZ Best was a "crime-owned" company. When I wasn't in the office, Ron Knox would come in and order Mike and Amy around, even telling them that *he owned the company.* And Lee was unhappy: Ron made it hard for him to speak with me unless he was present. My worst nightmare was becoming a reality—I was losing control.

❖ ❖ ❖

Donald Snyder called me from a pay phone on a Tuesday in late August. "Where's Ron?" he wanted to know.

"I don't know, Donald. But I've got your money. Do you want me to bring it to you?"

There was a long silence before he spoke again. "Yeah, kid, where do you want to meet?"

"Well, it's almost lunchtime . . . why don't we meet at Louie's?" I paused. "I'm buying," I added. "I'll meet you there in twenty minutes." Though I feared Donald, I couldn't see the harm in trying to get on his good side.

When I arrived, he was sitting at a table in a dark corner, away from the crowd. A lone candle provided illumination. Donald wasn't much for socializing.

"Been waiting long?"

"No, just got here. What's good here anyway?" he asked, studying the menu.

I glanced around and pushed a sealed envelope across the table. "It's all there, Donald. Twelve hundred and fifty dollars." He looked at me as if I had said something wrong. Hoping to correct myself, I blurted, "Uh, I usually get the barbecued ribs."

The expression on his face had changed. "How much did you say is in here?"

"Twelve fifty—that's what I've been paying Ron every week." He bowed his head and shook it slowly. "Was I supposed to pay more?"

"No, kid. I was only charging you a thousand a week. Ron marked it up on you and didn't bother telling me. That's going to cost him."

I felt my skin crawl. "Listen, Donald, I don't want any trouble. If he finds out I told you, he'll come after me."

"No, he won't. I'll make sure of it. . . . Just what is your arrangement with Ron?"

Because he seemed genuinely concerned, I told him every-thing—except that the jobs were phony. He heard me out and instructed me to say nothing to Ron.

"It's one thing to try and beat a guy like you," Donald said. "But to use my money to make a score behind my back without telling me—that's a different story. He'll pay, kid . . . you can bet on that."

"Is he going to give me trouble?" I asked, concerned.

Donald was out of patience. "Look, Barry, I told you I'll handle everything. Just pay me every Tuesday and take care of Lee by yourself. I'll do the rest. You got that?" He pointed across the table at my chest.

"I got it, Donald . . . I got it."

❖ ❖ ❖

True to his word, Donald settled matters with Ron—there was no sign of him. The Reseda employees were once again happy and content. Especially Amy and Mike. Although he didn't know why the sudden change had occurred, Lee enjoyed communicating with me directly. The rumors of my involvement with criminals behind the scenes also faded as company morale returned to normal.

With Ron no longer watching my every move, I decided to buy another car. A friend was selling a barely used, red Ferrari 308 for fifty-five thousand dollars. I put forty thousand down, took posses-sion of the car, and paid off the remaining fifteen on time.

The first day I drove it, I knew it was the car I'd always wanted. People from everywhere watched as I sped down the street. I cranked up the stereo and found temporary relief from my problems.

While I was showing off my new Ferrari around the San Fernando Valley, I wasn't worried about Ron Knox or Donald Snyder. But I should have been.

Ron's Back | 9

I've got to see you right away!" exclaimed a panicked Donald Snyder one Tuesday morning. "We've got problems." He told me to meet him in the parking lot of a library. The meeting was not optional.

Donald was standing by his car when I pulled my Ferrari into the busy lot. He saw me and walked toward my car.

"What's the problem?" I asked nervously as I slammed the door shut.

"It's about Ron."

"What about him?"

Usually Donald was calm and in control, but this time he was noticeably distraught. Something big was brewing. "Look, kid, I can't see you anymore."

"What do you mean you can't see me anymore? I've been making my payments on time, haven't I?"

"That has nothing to do with it. This guy Knox has some very good friends back east. He went to them about what happened between him and me over the money and they told us—me—to back off."

There was no love lost between Donald and me, but dealing with him was much easier than dealing with Ron. For one thing, Donald didn't think he owned my company. "Does that mean he's going to be hanging around me again?"

"I don't know what he's going to do. I talked to him this

morning, and he told me to have you meet him at Derrick's Diner in about an hour."

"What if I don't want him around anymore? What if I told these guys out east that I like you better? Don't I have any say in the matter?" I demanded angrily.

"You'll do as you're told!" he yelled. "And you won't cause any problems. You got that, kid?" He was staring at me intently. I had said too much.

"Yeah, I understand," I replied in a dejected tone and watched as Donald walked to his car, got in, and sped away.

❖   ❖   ❖

"Just coffee," I said to the waitress. I glanced at my watch— I was early. I tried to sort out in my mind just what Donald meant by "Ron's friends back east." Up until that morning, I had had no idea that people elsewhere in the country knew about or had any interest in ZZZZ Best.

I stared out the window at the car wash across the street and wished I were one of the minimum-wage workers busily wiping down each car. They weren't driving Ferraris, true, but they didn't have a Ron Knox in their lives, or his friends from out of town—whoever they were.

"I see you're on time," Ron said as he approached the table. I had been so preoccupied with the activities at the car wash that I hadn't seen him walk up. He slid into the booth and leveled his gaze at me. "Well, Barry, I hope you've learned your lesson." He smiled and made sure I was looking at him before he added pointedly, "No one gets away from Ron Knox."

"I've been paying everybody on time," I said, trying to change the subject. "Lee's people are happy, and the jobs are going smoothly."

"How's the Ferrari driving?" he asked sarcastically.

I wondered how he knew.

"Good," I said. "One of the few benefits from the restoration profits."

"Well then, you won't mind me asking for my profits from these jobs, will you?"

"No . . . when they're finished and we get paid, you'll get your forty thousand."

"Unfortunately, I can't wait that long. I have some associates who produce movies. They need money now to finish a project."

I knew I could get as much as I needed from Paul. I had good credit with him, so if Ron pressed me, I could come up with the money. But I wanted to stretch it out as long as I could.

"What kind of movie can be produced for forty thousand dollars?" I asked, stalling for time.

He sipped from his glass of ice water before answering. "A porno movie. We shoot them on video and then duplicate them. It's big business, kid, and I've got to have the forty thousand now!"

"All right, but I'll need two days to get an advance from Gary."

"I don't care how you get it. Just bring the money to my house in two days. I also want to pay off Donald and get rid of him. But that can wait until you finish the jobs."

"Anything else?"

"Yeah, one more thing. Have the Feds come to see you yet?"

"The Feds? Who are they?"

"The FBI. They'll probably visit you and ask a bunch of questions about me and my involvement with ZZZZ Best. I suggest you tell them that we have a legitimate arrangement. And whatever you do, say nothing about the financial statements or Donald's loan . . . understand?"

"I understand, Ron. They'll get nothing out of me," I promised.

"Good, kid." He smiled. "I knew you'd do what's best for you."

❖ ❖ ❖

Paul was more than happy to lend me as much as I wanted. He had grown accustomed to getting the weekly interest payments from me for over a year. I borrowed one hundred thousand dollars and paid off Ron and Donald. The rest I put in reserve, knowing the weekly interest payments to Lee and Paul would soon catch up with me. Even with his money, Ron had made it clear that I was still obligated to include him in all future restoration contracts. *There's just no getting rid of this guy,* I thought as I sat in my office.

The phone buzzed. It was Amy. "Barry, there's a Charles Hunter here to see you. Should I send him in?"

"You bet, Amy. Send him right in!" I said excitedly. Charlie Hunter had been a friend of mine for years, and right then I needed a friend.

I greeted him at the door. "Come on in, Charlie. What a surprise." He smiled and gave me a hug. "Can I get you some coffee?"

"No, Barry, I really don't have time. I just stopped by to talk to you for a few minutes."

"Sure, buddy. What's on your mind?"

Charlie slid his chair up to the desk and asked in a soft tone, "Are you in some kind of trouble, Barry?"

"Trouble? What do you mean?"

"You know I'm your friend. You can level with me. The word on the street is that you're involved with Ron Knox. Is that true?"

There was no reason for me to lie to Charlie. "Yeah, I'm involved with him," I answered reluctantly.

"Are you into him for some big money?"

"Not him personally, but I owe one hundred thousand dollars to a few people he introduced me to. . . . Why do you ask?"

Charlie glanced at the closed door. "The guy's no good,

Barry. He's a user. The only thing he wants from you is control of your company. And he'll stop at nothing until he gets it." Dumbfounded, I stared at Charlie. "You'll never get rid of the guy. He'll milk you dry . . . until there's nothing left."

"Great!" I stood and walked around the desk. "Is that what you came by to tell me? That I'm doomed?"

"No. I came to offer you some help."

"What kind of help?" The pressure was getting to me. I paced the office, rubbing my hands through my hair and fighting back tears. "According to you and everybody else, I should just kill myself before this maniac ruins me."

"Will you listen to me, Barry. I never told you this before, but I have a few friends who might be able to help you get rid of Knox. If you're interested, I want you to come by my house this Saturday and meet them."

"What good is that going to do? This Knox guy's got powerful friends back east who have an invisible shield around me," I moaned.

"If I didn't know for a fact that my people couldn't deliver you from Knox and his friends, I wouldn't be here."

Charlie was serious. And I needed help—desperately. "What time Saturday?"

"How about noon? Is that good for you?"

"Yeah," I said, turning to Charlie. "And thanks for saving my skin."

❖   ❖   ❖

Saturday morning usually afforded me an opportunity for some much-needed rest. The banks were closed, the week's interest payments had been made, and the pressures of running four offices had subsided by then. Still, I actually got more "normal" business done on the weekends than I did during the week.

I pulled into Charlie Hunter's neighborhood early that Saturday morning, looking for more than relief from Ron Knox. I was looking for the freedom to run ZZZZ Best the way I wanted. If Charlie's friend could provide that, I was a buyer.

After introductions and small talk, I took a chair at a table with Stanley Robbins, Robert Fuller, and Charlie. Stanley (he preferred "Stan"), a fortyish chain-smoker with a shock of brick-red hair, was quick-witted, funny, and according to Charlie, extremely well connected to important families back east. He owned several houses, including one in Florida. In the 1980s he'd bought a condominium in Southern California. He was a businessman—always looking for a good deal.

Robert Fuller was introduced to me as a "stock market whiz." Because of some of his past efforts, supposedly the Securities and Exchange Commission had been forced to change some of its procedures. Fuller was about sixty-five years old, heavyset, and had a strong personality, bordering on intimidating.

Stan was clearly in charge, though. When he talked, Charlie and Robert listened. He asked me simple questions about Knox: how we had met, how much Donald had lent me, who his contacts were, and what my current financial obligations to him were. I liked Stan. He seemed genuinely interested in helping me and expressed no desire to take over.

"If you don't tell me the whole truth, I can't help you, kid," Stan concluded.

I gave him *my* version of the "whole truth"—which, of course, excluded the phony restoration contracts.

Robert was more interested in the daily operations of ZZZZ Best: each location's monthly income, the number of employees I had, and my expansion plans.

After nearly two hours, the three men had a thorough understanding of my relationship with Ron Knox and how ZZZZ Best operated.

"You should be proud of yourself, Barry. You've built yourself a heck of a company," Stan said as he puffed on his cigarette. "And I'd like to help you out . . . but only if you want me to."

Everybody looked at me, awaiting a response. "I'd like you to help me, Stan. But how? Knox has me boxed in."

Stan paused. "You let me worry about that. If you want my help, I'm going to need your cooperation. You must do exactly what I say."

I was willing, but I needed to know more. "What would that entail?"

"First, you must cut off all communications with Knox. Don't accept his calls, and, whatever you do, don't call him."

"But what if he comes by the office? How do I ignore him then?"

"I'm going to need to bring one of my guys out from back east to hang out with you for about six months. He'll move in with you and follow you around wherever you go. That way if Knox tries anything, my guy will be there to . . . take care of business."

"Who is this guy?"

Stan glanced at Robert. "His name is Phil Cox. He's one of the toughest people I know. He'll be perfect for this job."

"Kind of like a bodyguard?"

"Yeah . . . you could say that . . . a bodyguard."

I liked the idea. Only important people had bodyguards. "How will I pay him?"

"Just put him on your payroll for eight hundred dollars a week. I'll take care of the rest. But it's important that he come out right away. If you want Knox to leave you alone, I need to get busy."

"Sounds fine to me, Stan."

"Good. Now, I'm not pushing you or anything, but I have a dear friend who has a financing company. I'm sure he can raise you all the money you need for these restoration projects— for a lot less than Knox's people are charging. You interested?"

This was too good to be true. Not only was I going to be delivered from Ron Knox, I was also being offered an unlimited amount of funds. "I'm very interested in that kind of deal," I said. "In fact, I'd be willing to split the profits with you on all the jobs you're able to arrange financing on."

"If that's what you want. But, remember, I didn't *force* you to make that deal." Charlie and Robert smiled at Stan's comment.

"I know," I replied. "I offered and I've got no regrets for doing so. Raising money has always been my biggest problem."

"Stan, can I add something?" Robert interjected. Stan nodded his approval. "Have you ever thought about taking your company public?" Robert asked me. "I mean, if raising money has been a problem for ZZZZ Best, it makes good business sense for you to consider going public."

I thought back to when Knox had mentioned the term *public,* but I still didn't know what it meant. And the last thing I wanted was to appear naive. "How long would it take for me to 'go public,' and how much money could I make?"

Silence again. My three new partners exchanged looks, struggling to communicate with each other with their eyes.

"I could probably get it done for you in about ninety days— around February," Robert replied. "As for the money you'll make, it really depends on how the deal is structured."

"You'll also have to hire a lawyer and an accountant to do the paperwork—but once that's done, you'll put ZZZZ Best in the big leagues," Stan added.

"That's right," Charlie said. "You'll be known all over the United States by those who purchase your stock."

"And since you're the sole owner of the company, you'll retain control because you'll be the majority stockholder," Robert said, emphasizing the point.

Whatever else going public meant, to me it meant fame, big money, and total control—everything I had ever wanted.

❖　❖　❖

"I love it, Barry!" Donna squealed as we toured the five-thousand-square-foot house in the new Westchester County Estates. "Can we please buy it?"

The broker had dropped the keys by my office. The two-story mansion boasted a huge living room, family room, and dining room, two fireplaces, a large kitchen, and even quarters for a live-in maid. After reviewing Carl Stowe's financial statements, the broker had assured me that if I put down $250,000, I could easily qualify for a loan to purchase the property. Although they were asking almost $800,000, I knew I could get it for $750,000.

Raising the down payment would be simple. I would use the money I received from Charlie and Stan to pay off Lee and Paul. Then I'd reborrow from them much more than that, using my flawless track record to support my request. Once I'd acquired the house and taken ZZZZ Best public, I would finally prove to everyone that I was a *big success*.

❖　❖　❖

When Phil Cox arrived on the scene, he looked the part of the typical hood. He wore dark sunglasses constantly in an attempt to hide a face that had been damaged on numerous occasions. He was not a large man but carried himself with confidence. He dressed neatly and I was told he carried a gun. Phil had earned a reputation as a legitimate tough guy through years of loyal service to people like Stan Robbins. We got along well, and I actually think he liked me. Most importantly, once the word got out on the street that he was living with me, Ron Knox stayed far away. To me, that was worth the eight hundred a week.

After several meetings with Stan, Charlie, and Robert, it was agreed that I would hire a securities lawyer known personally to Robert Fuller, and Roger Voss, a CPA from the midwest, to assist me in going public. They had worked together on previous deals and even though my company was two thousand miles away, they seemed eager to take on the new business.

We also made what came to be known as the big "stock score." ZZZZ Best would merge with a dormant, public company—a "shell company"—out of Salt Lake City. I would actually buy them out on paper, thereby automatically becoming public in the process. After secretly purchasing one million free-trading shares of that company's stock at five cents a share, right before the acquisition was announced, I was to split the shares up evenly among Stan, Charlie, Robert, and myself. Because they had several Wall Street "connections," who, according to them, would create a market for the stock, it wouldn't take long for the shares to increase in value dramatically.

We did this in conjunction with the financing being arranged for me at a company on the East Coast owned by an associate of Stan's. To keep the restoration projects separate from the stock deal and ZZZZ Best, we formed a company called Security Insurance Services. We leased office space where Charlie, Robert, and Stan would operate the business. Things were moving fast, even for my usual breakneck pace, but I didn't care. There was no turning back now.

❖ ❖ ❖

"Two gentlemen are here to see you, Barry," Amy said over the intercom. Before I had time to ask who these men were, she continued, "They're with the FBI."

My heart sank, but I didn't hesitate. "Send them in."

The two men, dressed in suits and carrying briefcases, entered the office and sat down across from my desk.

After brief introductions, one of them said, "Mr. Minkow, we're here to talk to you about your relationship with Ron Knox. You do know him, don't you?"

Knox had warned me at Derrick's Diner that the FBI might visit, but I hadn't believed him. I was scared and caught off guard. "Yes, I know him," I answered calmly, trying not to raise suspicion.

"Well, Mr. Minkow, the word on the street is that he's 'shaking you down' pretty good through some steep loans." They watched to see if I would react. I didn't, but I recalled that Charlie had heard the same rumor.

"Look, Mr. Minkow, you're not a target of our investigation. We know this Knox guy has infiltrated ZZZZ Best, and we want to help you get rid of him," one of them added.

Did these men know about Fuller, Robbins, and Hunter? I wondered. If they didn't ask about them, I wasn't going to offer any information. I worded my response carefully. "Assuming that what you say is true, how could you guys help me?"

"We want you to testify in front of a federal grand jury about your business dealings with Ron Knox. If you cooperate, we can put this guy away for a long time."

So, they weren't aware of the phony restoration contracts or my new relationship with Stan and his friends. They were preoccupied with Ron Knox. That was fine with me.

After asking a few more questions and showing me several photos to see if I could identify various individuals, they left their cards and promised to keep in touch. I immediately called Charlie and Robert at the Security offices and told them about my surprise visitors. They were satisfied with the way I had handled the interview and gave me explicit instructions to let them know whenever the FBI contacted me again.

❖ ❖ ❖

November and December of 1985 were busy months for ZZZZ Best. We opened our fifth office in Santa Barbara, increasing the number of employees to almost two hundred. To keep pace with the growth, I hired additional office personnel, purchased several computers, and leased more space in the Reseda Business Center. I worked daily with the securities lawyer and Roger Voss, gathering the information they needed to complete the merger.

Gary Todd and I decided it was time to place some of the phony restoration contract paperwork under a different company. With so many "investors" having Partner letterhead with Gary's name on it, he feared getting caught. So we opened a small, one-man office across town, had letterhead printed, and made it the official headquarters of Reliable Appraisal Company—an independent adjusting company owned and operated by Gary Todd.

With the burden of chasing after funds lifted, I was now able, for the first time in my business career, to focus the majority of my time on ZZZZ Best. I hired a public-relations firm to get the biggest bang for my publicity buck. At nineteen, I was about to be the president of a public company. This was big news, and I wanted *everyone* to know about it.

The employees at the Reseda office quickly became accustomed to seeing Phil hanging around. He was quiet and stayed out of the way, which made my life much better than in the days when Knox had been in my life. And when I moved into my new $750,000 home, Phil and Donna moved in with me.

❖ ❖ ❖

"Sit down, 'Wonder Boy,'" Stan said as I approached the table at Alex's Restaurant, where he had asked me to meet him to discuss Ron Knox. As usual, Robert and Charlie were with him.

"Everything's set with the loan company," he said. "Within ninety days, you'll have five hundred thousand dollars, and by May, you'll have a two-million-dollar credit line available."

"That's great, Stan!" I didn't try to hide my excitement.

"There's one catch. It's going to cost you a fifty-thousand-dollar kicker on the five hundred thousand and two hundred fifty thousand on the two million. Can you handle that?"

"No problem, Stan. I'll give the money to Robert once the loan comes through, and we'll be set."

"Good. I've got to leave for New York next week, but I'll be back. You're in good hands, so don't worry about anything."

"Is everything set for January on the merger?" I asked.

"Yes, it is," Robert interjected. "But as soon as the deal closes, Roger Voss needs to come out and start working on a year-end audit. . . . Are your earnings good?"

The correct answer to that question was, "Who knows?" With all the loans, kickbacks, and car payments, I had no way of knowing exactly how the offices were doing. I had to lie. "Yeah, every office is making a profit. Even Santa Barbara is doing well, and it just opened."

There was silence at the table as the three men thought about my remarks.

"By the way, kid, Knox is going to sue you," Stan said at last.

"*What?*"

"Apparently the guy is desperate for money. But don't worry. We've talked to our people back east, and they told us that if he sues, you're free to do whatever you have to in order to protect yourself."

"What does that mean exactly?"

"That means that we're going to get you a lawyer we can trust to defend you. If he thinks it's a good idea for you to testify against Knox, we'll let you—as long as you say the right things."

I had a lot to hide and wasn't too keen on going before a grand jury. But I didn't want them to know that. "However you want to handle it is fine with me. When will the suit be filed?"

"Any day now. But just forget about it. Give it to Robert, and he'll set up a meeting with the lawyer."

"Is it safe for me to travel from office to office, or will I have to be constantly looking over my shoulder for Knox?" I asked, trying to stifle the ripple of fear that tingled down my spine.

Stan smiled. "It's safe. . . . Just make sure you take Phil wherever you go." He pointed toward the restaurant rest rooms, where Phil was leaning against the wall, watching my every move.

❖ ❖ ❖

"ZZZZ Best Taken Public by 19-Year-Old Founder." This headline blazed from the business section of the paper early in 1986. The news brought an onslaught of inquiries from across the country. My public-relations firm had to work overtime to keep up with the requests.

Robert had proved himself to be an expert at generating interest in ZZZZ Best stock. Just weeks before the deal closed, he flew to New York and persuaded several brokerage firms to create a market for our stock, and the stock rose from five to fifty cents a share in two weeks! Since I was the majority stockholder, that made me worth millions—on paper. I had learned that some securities law prohibited me from selling any of my six million personal shares, gained through the merger, for two years. But I could sell the 250,000 shares of free-trading stock from our four-way split—as long as no one found out about it.

Becoming a public company dramatically increased morale at ZZZZ Best. We had accomplished something the competition could only dream of, a point I reinforced at weekly company meetings: "So, who would you rather work for: ZZZZ Best, a company that will one day be the General Motors of the carpet-cleaning industry, or some loser local company that's going nowhere fast?"

As news spread of my goal to one day go nationwide, carpet cleaners from several companies tried to join the ZZZZ Best team. What a difference from a year earlier, when I had worried about the competition stealing my people!

❖   ❖   ❖

I was in a buoyant mood one late January day when my Mom knocked on the office door. I lived in a beautiful home, drove a Ferrari, and controlled a public company—all at the age of nineteen. She was probably coming to congratulate me.

I invited her in, smiling broadly. "What's on your mind, Ma?"

"Oh, just thought I'd stop by and say hi since you haven't had much time for your father and me lately," she said sadly.

"Sorry about that, Mom, but I'm busy. I've got almost two hundred employees and stockholders all over the country," I reminded her.

"I know, son, and I'm very proud of you." I could see that she was disturbed about something. "But what happens when ZZZZ Best goes nationwide? Then what? Will you be satisfied then?"

An interesting word—*satisfied*. And it got my attention. I wasn't satisfied unless I was expanding or accomplishing something. And even then the satisfaction didn't last.

"I don't know, Mom. Guess I'll have to do it and find out." I was smiling. But she wasn't. She was concerned about my fast-paced lifestyle and the future.

Then, out of nowhere, she asked me a question that I'll never forget: "Is all this money of yours going to buy you a ticket to heaven?"

My usually quick-witted mind was temporarily stumped as I struggled to respond.

Back in 1975, Mom had become a born-again Christian,

and our Jewish family had constantly persecuted her for her belief in Jesus Christ. She was told not to "preach" to us as we grew up. Nonetheless, she still read her Bible and prayed all the time. Although I had gone to temple for years, my faith in God was minimal at best. As far as I could tell, He had never appeared to respond to my desperate prayers for financial help with ZZZZ Best, nor had He cared about my daily circumstances. Besides, I was making too much money to feel that I needed anyone— even God. And at my age, the prospect of heaven seemed very far away.

I'll never forget my response to my mother, an answer that summarized my feelings about God and heaven: "Mom, how much is God? I'll buy him." Needless to say, she left the room, unimpressed and unamused.

As I sat there thinking about her question, I wondered if there really was a "God" out there. And if there was, would He want anything to do with a guy who lied, cheated, and stole every day? Maybe I'd look into it after I became rich and famous.

Financial Frenzy 10

W hat's my temperature now?" I asked the nurse.

"You're down to about ninety-nine and a half," she said. "That's pretty good, Barry, but you can't go home until the doctor sees you."

"But I'm much better!" I insisted. I didn't have time for this. I had a public company to oversee and a lawsuit to fight. "Just give me some medicine and I'll be fine."

"Mr. Minkow, you've just recovered from a traumatic high fever. You're still on an IV! Just wait for the doctor . . . okay?" She was too pretty to argue with.

I'd been hospitalized for dehydration resulting from vomiting and an elevated body temperature. The steroids had so damaged my immune system that my body couldn't fight off a common cold. But I didn't tell the doctor I was taking steroids; to him, my problems were "stress-related." For some reason, I had to keep taking them. If I couldn't walk into the gym at any time and bench press over 350 pounds, I'd feel weak, insecure, and defenseless.

After spending one more day in the hospital, the doctor allowed me to return to my hectic pace. Gone only four days, I had a lot of catching up to do when I stepped into my office at ZZZZ Best headquarters. Perpetrating such a large fraud required all my time.

First, I created more phony restoration contracts—complete

In uniform at Ridgewood Military Academy.

My early childhood was spent in the Jewish faith.

I was sixteen when I started ZZZZ Best.

Me celebrating my ninteenth birthday.

My mother was a constant source of encouragement.

Joyce (in middle) with my two sisters, Gail and Sheri.

I loved having barbeques at my house!

Two lovely women in my life—Joyce and my grandmother.

Mom and Dad at a ZZZZ Best awards ceremony.

Posing for a TV commercial in 1987.

The fruits of labor—my beautiful red Ferarri.

I played quarterback on the inmate team at Lompoc.

with verification letters from Gary—to justify the loans I was receiving through Stan, Robert, and Charlie. Their money-raising efforts, though formidable, never seemed to go far enough. The interest payments depleted whatever cash surplus I had accumulated, and I was faced with another cash crunch. Also Robert, Stan, and Charlie asked to be put on my payroll—a "hiring" that cost me thousands a month.

To stay ahead of commitments, I embarked upon a multi-pronged, all-out borrowing spree: I reborrowed from Lee, Julie, and several of their friends—despite specific instructions not to from Stan and company. I approached banks, hoping that since ZZZZ Best was now a public company, I'd qualify for loans. And I did! Three different banks all lent me money, either personally or through ZZZZ Best.

With the assistance of Jerry Williams, I also figured out a way to defraud leasing companies. The deal worked like this: Between February and July of 1986, I asked several leasing companies to loan ZZZZ Best money to buy equipment. I told them that Jerry, who was an authorized distributor for Benson Equipment, was selling me specially made units—the Benson Super Cleaner—for $4,500 each and available only through him. There were no such machines. To strengthen the ruse, Jerry agreed to buy back the nonexistent machines if I failed to pay. The leasing companies made out the checks to Benson Equipment. Jerry skimmed a percentage, gave me the balance, and ZZZZ Best made the payments on the leases.

I used the proceeds from the bank loans and leases to open two additional ZZZZ Best locations: Lancaster in March and San Bernardino in April. Robert had told me that if I wanted the stock to go up, I had to "make things happen," like opening more locations (even though the company wasn't strong enough to support them). He was right. By my twentieth birthday, the stock had soared to almost three dollars a share.

This made aging easier for me. I had accomplished something in my twentieth year that, as far as I knew, no one else my age had accomplished in the history of American business: I ran a public company while still under the age of twenty-one. That was newsworthy enough to feed my ego and keep me in the limelight for at least two more years.

But when it came time to make payments, my cash victories evaporated. I needed to raise money that *I didn't have to pay back!* Selling my undisclosed 250,000 free-trading shares was my only option. But before I could do that, I needed approval "from the top," and that meant a meeting with Stan.

❖ ❖ ❖

"We've got nearly three hundred employees, seven locations, and ten restoration projects going, Stan! That's why I need the money!" I said from the backseat of Robert's limousine, parked near a restaurant.

"I can probably get John Brady and somebody else to buy them," Robert said calmly. "That would keep the sale from putting too much pressure on the stock."

John was a stockbroker Robert knew. When Robert said "Buy," John and other brokers asked, "How much?" Robert had a lot of influence on Wall Street.

"I think the kid's not telling us something," Stan stated pointedly to Robert and Charlie. "I think he's probably giving money to someone he hasn't told us about yet. Is that true, kid?" he demanded. Stan never asked a question he didn't already know the answer to. There was a long silence.

Charlie had asked me for two hundred thousand dollars to buy some property. I advanced him the money against future profits from the restoration projects, swearing never to tell Stan or Robert about the loan. I tried to resist the temptation to make eye contact with Charlie, but failed. Stan was too "street smart"; he saw right through the deal.

"Charlie, where'd you get the money to buy that land?" Stan asked loudly. He was angry. There was another long pause. I had blown it. "Well, I'm waiting!"

"Look, Stan," I interjected, trying to change the subject, "I promise that everything will be okay—as soon as I sell this stock. You, Robert, and Charlie can keep your shares. I'm only asking to sell mine."

"What's the status of the Knox lawsuit?" Stan asked Robert.

"I've got a lawyer for the kid now. He understands the delicate nature of the situation. We're going to have Barry cooperate against this guy with the Feds," Robert replied.

Stan nodded, apparently satisfied with the answer, then turned to me. "Have the 'Fibbies' been to see you again, Barry?"

"Yeah, one of the men came by again—this time with somebody new. They said the same thing as before: 'We know Knox is extorting money from you and wants to continue to do so. Help us and you won't be sorry'—that kind of thing, Stan."

"Did you mention any of us?" he questioned.

"No!"

"Did *they* ask about us?"

"No. They're so focused on Knox that nothing else matters."

"Good." His attention shifted to Fuller. "Robert, sell the shares in blocks. I don't want any pressure on this stock, so take your time and do it right."

"No problem, Stan. I'll take care of it immediately," Robert responded.

"Anything else, kid?" Stan asked.

"Not right now, but I'll keep you posted," I replied, thankful that the inquisition was over.

"All right, you can leave." As I climbed out of the car, Charlie was right behind me. "But *you stay*," Stan said to Charlie pointedly. "We've got something to discuss."

❖ ❖ ❖

"It's time for you to make some big money, Gary," I said. "I want you to go full time with Reliable, and I'm willing to finance the expansion." I had no other option. It was only a matter of time before Gary Todd would get caught confirming nonexistent restoration jobs.

As he sat in my office that spring afternoon, I could tell that he was thinking about the fringe benefits of running his company, full time. "What's your timing on this transition?" he asked me.

"I want you to do it now. I'll give you the money for everything you need."

"What would be my responsibilities?"

"Good question." I stood up and paced the office. "It's really twofold. First, you'll verify all ZZZZ Best contracts. Second, I want you to try to legitimize these restoration projects by actually obtaining some real insurance business and assigning it to ZZZZ Best."

"I doubt I'll ever be able to substantiate millions of dollars worth of jobs," he objected.

I raised my hand. "That's not what I'm after. I just want you to get us *some* real work, and keep my investors satisfied. You got the idea?" I said, smiling.

Gary paused, thinking it over. "How many employees will you let me hire?"

"I don't care. Hire as many as you want. If they can bring in business, hire 'em! I'll cover the payrolls."

He was sold. "Cut me a check so I can get started, and I'll have a functioning office ready within a week."

❖ ❖ ❖

"Carl Stowe, you are a hard man to track down," I said as the two of us talked in my second-story office.

Carl was a tall, thin man of about forty-five, and extremely intense. We had been introduced through Ron Knox and had kept in touch ever since. Whenever I needed phony financial statements or tax returns, Carl delivered—for a price, of course. He also occasionally tried to raise money for ZZZZ Best, but was never successful. It may have been this lack of success that showed him just how phony ZZZZ Best really was. Though I never initially told him the whole truth about my relationship with Ron Knox and the restoration projects, he saw through everything—and of course he'd been preparing all the doctored financials. I liked Carl. He knew I was a fraud, but he still admired what I had accomplished at ZZZZ Best.

"I keep busy, Barry. I've got to make a living somehow," he said jokingly.

My decision to increase Carl's involvement in the company was based on his accounting expertise. I needed a certified audit from Roger Voss and didn't have the time nor the ability to create the necessary paperwork. Carl was someone I could trust and confide in. No longer was it Barry Minkow versus Knox, Fuller, Robbins, Cox, Hunter, Lee, Paul, Jerry, the banks and auditors. Now it was Barry and Carl.

"Carl, I have here a list from Roger Voss that details all the documents he must have to complete the audit. As you know, you need to create most of the stuff." I handed him the three-page letter and gave him time to look it over. "Stan and Robert want this audit completed no later than August."

"Who are they, and how do they fit into ZZZZ Best?"

Although I trusted Carl, that information was on a need-to-know basis. Not wanting to raise suspicion, I downplayed the relationship. "They're just friends who helped take me public. There's absolutely nothing to worry about with them. They're pulling for us."

He seemed relieved. "Good. Well, it's going to take me a few weeks to create all these bank statements and documents, but I can get it done. I also need to go meet with Roger a few times to explain things."

"That's fine with me. How soon can you get started?"

"Right away . . . but I've got one question. Let's say we pass the audit—then what?" He paused. "I mean, where's the cure? You can't just keep borrowing from Peter to pay off Paul and expect to survive. One day it's going to catch up to you."

Carl was right, except for one thing. I pulled open the top drawer of my desk, took out my ZZZZ Best stock certificates, and handed them to him. "By January of 1988, these shares will become free-trading. My plan is to survive until then; sell a million shares at, say, ten dollars a share; and then pay everybody off once and for all. If I can keep things going until then, I'll be able to solve all my problems and make you a very wealthy man."

Carl was impressed. I did have an "ultimate goal," and it included putting an end to ridiculous interest on loans and phony restoration contracts. "Well, if we need to survive for another eighteen months or so, I'd better get busy." He left the office.

❖ ❖ ❖

"Hello?" I said groggily into the phone. The clock on my nightstand said 2:30.

"Barry, is that you? It's Robert." He sounded panicked.

"Yeah, what's up?"

"It's Charlie. They beat him up pretty good."

"Who did?"

"I can't tell you over the phone, but Stan called and wanted me to make sure that you don't talk to or meet with Charlie anymore. Do you understand?"

I hated Robert's condescending use of that phrase. "Yeah, I understand. Who did it?"

He didn't answer my question. "That's not your concern. Just run the company and do as we tell you." He hung up.

❖ ❖ ❖

June and July were busy months. Mike and I traveled frequently to all seven ZZZZ Best locations, trying to boost sales and build mature management. Business was good, considering we had expanded much too quickly. And we wanted to expand again, into northern California, by no later than July. The more locations we opened, the easier it was for Robert to "hype up" the stock by likening ZZZZ Best to 7–11 convenience stores. And it worked. The stock soon soared to over four dollars a share.

Carl Stowe was doing well with Roger Voss. Whenever Voss requested more information, Carl was quick to respond. The audit would be completed on time.

To verify the restoration projects, Carl used the Reliable Appraisal Company's letterhead provided by Gary Todd. Gary had established the insurance adjusting company and had hired three adjusters and a secretary, who was instructed on how to handle all ZZZZ Best-related calls.

The cash demands and weekly expenses of a company with over 325 employees pushed me toward two additional investors. One of them set up a $1-million loan for ZZZZ Best at a bank in Los Angeles. A executive in the oil business who enjoyed investing in profitable ventures also signed on. I told them I needed the money to complete restoration projects, for which they would receive 50 percent of the contract profits. With their funds I opened our first northern California office and put a big dent in the $2-million loan Stan had set up for me.

By the summer of 1986, Charlie Hunter had been replaced by Alan Hoffman, a man supposedly "well connected." According to Robert, Alan "had a lot of juice" and supervised a lot of "family business" in California. Phil had known Alan for some time and "trusted him with his life." To me, he was a nice, quiet man who never boasted of his influence and always treated me with respect.

The first thing Alan did was handle Ron Knox by showing Ron's friends from back east canceled checks proving that I had paid Knox over five hundred thousand dollars. After midsummer 1986 Ron Knox was out of my life—forever! Though this was a tremendous victory, it didn't help my cash crunch.

About this time one of my associates told me he knew how to raise fifteen million dollars that I wouldn't have to pay back. An investment banking firm could do it through a public stock offering. He explained the difference between ZZZZ Best going public through a merger (as we had done in January of 1986) and actually selling shares and receiving the proceeds. The idea appealed to me. Fifteen million dollars would help me pay off the two-million dollar loan, Lee Herring, and Paul Weaver, and would cover all my other expenses. But the clincher for me was the prospect of a statewide television advertising campaign—including commercials in which I would star.

But first I had to get approval from my business partners. Without Stan Robbin's blessing, I couldn't do anything. Not wanting to discuss such matters over the phone, I drove out to Stan's condominium. Stan was holding court at the dining room table in his normal attire—pants with no shirt or shoes, and a cigarette in his hand. He was blowing smoke rings. A large audience—mostly longtime friends visiting from the east—was in attendance, listening to him spin tales from his past.

I got the usual welcome as I entered the room: "Hey, Stan, the whiz kid's here." But I wasn't in the mood for laughs. I needed Stan to approve the public offering and provide buying power for the stock through his East Coast connections. Unfortunately, he was so preoccupied with his friends that I was having trouble getting his ear. So I decided to shift his focus to me. I took off my shirt and shoes and sat down next to Stan. Then I snatched up one of his cigarettes, lit it, and puffed away. There we were, two shirtless wheeler-dealers sitting around a table smoking cigarettes. The guys loved it. It worked—I had Stan's full attention.

I gave him an abridged version of the deal, while he listened attentively. When I had finished, he looked me right in the eye and said, "You're crazy, kid. But that's why I like you so much. And since this deal means so much to you, I'm going to let you do it."

I gave him a big hug and the traditional kiss on the cheek and put my shirt and shoes back on.

Just before I got out the door, Stan said one more thing: "Just don't let me down!"

I drove home that evening with Stan's final warning in my mind. In order to keep my word to Stan and to my 325 employees, I'd have to pull off the biggest con of my life. This would be much harder than my other cons because Wall Street pros would investigate my claims about ZZZZ Best.

But they were going to meet their match. By this time— the end of July 1986—I was a seasoned con man with years of experience in deceiving and manipulating. With the company on the line and my secret partners looking over my shoulder, I would do whatever it took to get the deal done.

Financial Fix?

S o, what's the balance in my business checking account?" I asked from the car phone, en route to one of the biggest business meetings of my young life.

"You've got $152,800, and after we pay today's checks, you'll have $22,900!"

Must be all those payroll checks clearing at once, I thought.

"Okay, and thank you very much for your help. By the way, did you get the candy I sent you?"

"Yes, Barry, I did. And thanks. I'm the talk of the bank!" she said proudly.

The woman deserved more than candy. She always alerted me ahead of time whenever my business checking account was overdrawn. In a critical position, she was able to give me immediate credit on large checks, which allowed me, on occasions (unbeknownst to her), to float funds through an elaborate check-kiting scheme.

"I'll be making another deposit tomorrow at about ten o'clock. You'll be there, won't you?"

"Of course."

"Look forward to seeing you then. 'Bye for now," I said in my sweetest voice. I hung up the car phone and slapped both hands against the steering wheel. There was only $22,900 left in the account. The weekly cash demands were catching up to me— again. I needed the funds from the public offering to keep afloat until that wonderful day in January of 1988 when I could sell some of my stock and pay everyone off, permanently.

Big meetings were no problem for me. By now I was a skilled con man who could lie to anyone, anywhere, at any time, under any conditions. This meeting was with a banker named Howard Kane. Kane had been impressed by the bogus financial statements and other information about the company I sent him. That was good. But something bothered me about meeting with him. Maybe it was because he had flown all the way from the East Coast just to see me. Or perhaps it was dawning on me that if I didn't convince him to raise the fifteen million dollars, ZZZZ Best would go under. I simply owed too many people too much money.

Leaving the freeway, I headed for our 12:30 P.M. lunch meeting. I had time for one last call.

"Hello," said the stressed voice on the other end of the line.

"Well, Carl, this is it. This is the big cure!" I said. "If we pull this one off, I can stop kiting checks and worrying about having enough cash to meet our expenses."

"Just think, Barry, with fifteen million dollars, you won't need to depend on people like Lee Herring and Paul Weaver anymore. This can almost be a normal business!"

I laughed and got down to business. "Listen, we're going to have to make another deposit tomorrow, so get things ready."

"No problem," he replied. "Are you ready for the big meeting? We've got a lot riding on it."

He didn't need to remind me. "I'll be fine, my friend," I said, full of confidence. "You just make sure the checks don't bounce, and I'll handle the rest."

"I just didn't want you to get cold feet. After all, we're in the big leagues now—*Wall Street*. Get it?" he said enthusiastically.

"Yeah, I got it." I thought for a moment. He was right. This would be the biggest con of my life. "Don't forget, Carl, we're not raising this money to run to Europe and leave everybody stuck with the bills. We're going to meet payrolls, pay back investors, and develop a legitimate and profitable company. And if that happens, everybody's a winner and nobody gets hurt." I said this more to assure myself than Carl.

"You don't have to convince me," he replied. "I'm with you all the way . . . to make sure we survive until January of 1988. Once everybody gets paid and there are no victims, then there will have been no crime." The relief was evident in his voice.

"Right on, Carl!" My conscience was temporarily appeased. "Hey, I just pulled up to the restaurant. Take it easy, man."

"Good luck!" were his final words.

I tossed the valet my keys and made my way to the entrance, the hot July sun burning against my three-piece suit. I much preferred tank tops and shorts, but for fifteen million dollars, I was willing to dress up. The maitre d' led me to a table on the outside patio. Mr. Kane was early.

After we had made our introductions and placed our orders, Howard Kane smiled and said, "So, why should I raise all this money for you, Mr. Minkow?"

"Because I'm building the nation's largest carpet-and furniture-cleaning and restoration company. And by raising ZZZZ Best the funds we need, you'll be on the ground floor of a guaranteed winner." It was amazing how easy it had become for me to lie.

"Is that so?" he replied. "Tell me what you would do with an influx of fifteen million dollars."

I paused long enough for him not to suspect that I had a well-rehearsed answer. "Well, Mr. Kane, to begin with, I want to open ten new carpet-cleaning stores. Each will cost approximately $250,000 to start, but will be profitable within sixty days. We know this based on the eight offices that are already open and functioning. I also want to use about $7 million to buy materials and supplies for our ongoing restoration business. If I can finance 100 percent of these jobs, I'll no longer need partners and investors. This will increase my profitability tremendously, because I won't have to give up half my action." I allowed him to absorb what I had said. "Additionally, the company will invest $4 million in a massive television advertising campaign that will dramatically increase our commercial and residential penetration in the marketplace. The balance of the funds will be used for working capital." As I spoke, I never took my eyes off his face.

"Those are ambitious goals," he said as he sipped from his glass. "Do you have the management to back you up?"

"Yes, I do. My policy has always been to promote from within. Every one of our current managers started out as carpet cleaners or phone solicitors and worked their way up. My people know we are in the process of building a massive empire, and they want to grow with the company."

He nodded in approval, and I warmed to my subject. "My policy with personnel is simple, Mr. Kane. We're going places at ZZZZ Best and our track record proves it. We continue to open new carpet-cleaning locations every other month, and company morale is at an all-time high. People from other companies would give their right arm to be a part of our management team because they want to be with a winner," I said excitedly. He was listening attentively.

"Well, Mr. Minkow, it seems that you've done your homework. But going public isn't easy. I've got to hire lawyers who will investigate your company thoroughly. It will take about four months to put together a prospectus, and then you'll need to fly all over the country to present your company to the investment community. Are you ready for that kind of commitment?"

The word *investigate* always scared me. The last thing I needed was a pack of Wall Street lawyers I didn't know, diligently examining my company for four months. But I had no choice, if I wanted to keep ZZZZ Best—and myself—alive.

Knowing that the best defense is a good offense, I boldly stated, "Of course I am. I wouldn't be here wasting your time if I wasn't prepared to invest all my efforts into the deal. When do we get started?''

His smile told me that he was convinced. "I'll make a few calls when I get back east and have my lawyers contact you immediately. I'll also want you to fly out in a few weeks and meet some of the stockbrokers who will help sell the deal."

"Sounds great!" I replied. "Are we agreed on fifteen million?"

Mr. Kane did not hesitate. "I'm in agreement with that figure. Just do your part and get through the four months of constant meetings with lawyers, auditors, and investigators, and I'll worry about raising the funds."

"You've got a deal." I stuck out my hand to seal it.

"Deal." Mr. Kane shook my hand.

We raised our glasses and toasted the success of ZZZZ Best. The rest of the time was spent answering the usual inquiries about how I got started in the carpet-cleaning industry at such a young age.

After lunch, I headed straight back to my office. Carl Stowe was waiting for me.

"We've got it, buddy!" I announced jubilantly. "Fifteen million dollars!"

Carl pounded his fist against my desk. "Right on, man!" he shouted, then quickly sobered. "But what do we need to do to get it?" Carl had had enough experience in raising money to know that even the smallest of bank loans required huge amounts of paperwork.

"Relax, my friend," I said reassuringly. "All we need to do is satisfy these Wall Street big shots and we've got the money!"

The expression on Carl's face reflected doubt. "I don't know, Barry. If going public were easy, everybody'd be doing it. These guys might not fall for the restoration con."

"Carl, listen to me!" I got out of my chair and walked to his side of the desk. "I've been waiting for the one big deal that would solve all my financial problems since the days in the garage. And I'll be darned if I'm going to let a bunch of Wall Street stuffed shirts stand in the way of my only opportunity to get all of these people off my back!"

He could see the determination in my eyes and allowed my words to sink in before asking, "How long will this whole going-public process take?"

"From start to finish, four months. But that's four months of intense meetings, tons of paperwork, and a significant amount of traveling. For fifteen million dollars, I'm willing to put up with it." I leveled a searching look at him. "How about you?"

"You know where I stand, Barry—right next to you, all the way!"

I filled Carl in on the rest of the details. By the time we had finished, we were ready to take on Wall Street.

❖ ❖ ❖

Howard Kane's first demand was that I obtain highly-respected law and accounting firms. I followed his recommendations and hired a nationally recognized law firm and an internationally known accounting firm. David Lundy, of a high-powered East Coast law firm, was placed in charge of my deal. He was a likable, intelligent man who never forgot a detail. When talking to him about the company, I had to watch my words carefully so I wouldn't contradict myself. I spent a great deal of time with David in the following months—perhaps too much, because I was beginning to like him as a friend and felt guilty for lying to him about ZZZZ Best.

Matt Paulson was in charge of the project for the accounting firm. Although serious, Matt was easy to talk to, but he was very thorough and seemed always to be asking for one more document relating to the restoration projects.

While I courted Kane, Lundy, and Paulson, Carl Stowe created volumes of documents to substantiate our restoration business. He made up invoices from suppliers that didn't exist. He reconciled bank statements and tied them into ledgers so that the company appeared to be making big profits. By using blank checks from Reliable Appraisal Company, Carl even made it look like Gary Todd's company had paid ZZZZ Best millions of dollars.

Gary also did his part. When the Wall Street lawyers or the accounting people called Reliable, he provided good recommendations and verified ZZZZ Best's contracts.

Meanwhile, carpet-cleaning sales were up. Mike increased our residential business by successfully opening three new locations: two in northern California and the other in Monrovia. This pushed our total employees to well over four hundred.

The rapid expansion, coupled with the pressure of going public, forced me to put in fifteen-hour days. My health suffered greatly as a result. I continued taking steroids all the same, fighting a never-ending battle to retain my strength.

Robert, Stan, Alan, and Phil placed few demands on me during these busy months. The frequent meetings at Stan's condominium dropped off to once or twice a week. It was in their interest that I complete the public offering. After all, Stan and Robert still owned half a million shares of free-trading ZZZZ Best stock that I had purchased for them at five cents a share.

❖ ❖ ❖

"I won't be home 'til about 4:00 A.M., Donna," I said into my car phone. "I'll be at the financial printer all night, putting the final touches on the public offering."

"Do you want me to wait up for you?" she asked kindly.

I laughed. "Of course not! Go on to sleep. By the time you wake up tomorrow morning, ZZZZ Best will be an official Wall Street success."

"How's your stomach feeling? Have you been throwing up blood today?"

"No. I'm all right," I lied. I leaned over to the rearview mirror of my BMW and studied my face. The streetlights exposed dark rings under my eyes. *Steroids are no substitute for sleep,* I said to myself.

"When this deal's done, can we spend more time together?" she asked. Donna enjoyed all the new cars and the house in Westchester County Estates, but she wasn't seeing much of me.

"Yes, honey," I replied immediately. "But after the completion of this offering, I'll be forced to travel more."

"Can't I go with you?" she pressed.

I didn't want to make any promises I couldn't keep. Traveling was an opportunity to spend time with other women. It's what every business executive did—so I thought. "We'll see, honey. . . . Listen, I've got to go now. I'm almost at the printer's. I love you."

"I love you too," she said in a disappointed tone.

I arrived at the printer at 10:00 P.M. The cool December air helped perk me up. I waved to Phil who was following me closely in his own car, and watched him park half a block down the street. *If Matt Paulson and David Lundy knew I had a live-in bodyguard who had a questionable past, they'd never do business with me,* I thought as I walked in the main entrance.

The place reminded me of a high-class hotel. The waiting room was beautifully furnished with velvet sofas and chairs. Original paintings hung on the walls, and the carpets didn't have a spot on them! When the staff realized I was the company president, they treated me like a king, escorting me down a long, well-lit corridor. Brass baseboards sparkled, reflecting the recessed ceiling lights. This was like no other printing company I had ever seen.

We finally arrived at a large conference room for this one last meeting with the lawyers and accountants. As usual, everyone was there ahead of me. A large table covered with documents dominated the room. David Lundy, Matt Paulson, and several other people from their firm were joined by the other lawyers and investment company executives. Each had the task of proof-reading the final prospectus before it went to print and making all necessary final revisions.

Watching all this gave me a feeling of power. Lawyers and accountants flown in from the East Coast, a score of adjutants bustling about, a printing facility rented for many thousands of dollars an hour—all of this because of me. I'd overcome many obstacles to get here, and I wasn't about to let this moment of glory pass without basking in it. Banks couldn't stop me, back room crooks couldn't stop me, even the Wall Street big shots with their Harvard degrees couldn't stop me from taking ZZZZ Best from a garage to a multi-million-dollar public company.

A second glance around the room revealed a basket of fresh fruit hidden amongst the papers on the conference table. Most of the men in the group had loosened their ties and rolled up their sleeves. It was late; only those in the big leagues knew about all-night meetings at financial printers. I made my way to the fruit basket.

"Well, look who's here." said a voice from the crowd. Everyone stopped what they were doing and greeted me.

"I'm glad you're finally here," said David Lundy. "We've got a lot to do." I shook a few hands on the way to my seat. "Okay, Barry, here's what's happening. We're all reviewing each page of the prospectus one last time. After we've made final revisions, you'll be given each page for approval, and then we'll give it to the printer." David loved to give instructions.

"Where's the printing press?" I asked naively.

"Out these doors to your left," David replied. "You're spending $200,000 in this place, and they haven't given you a tour?"

"I've been busy," I said. "Besides, you're the one who referred me here." We smiled.

I'd never before seen anything like a financial printing operation. With their high-tech equipment, they had the capacity to produce thousands of full-color, glossy prospectuses and distribute them nationally via air in a matter of hours. This was definitely the big leagues. No one needed this kind of service unless he was raising major dollars.

It took four hours to go through the prospectus. Even though it was late, I was too keyed up to be tired. I thought about walking into the bank with millions of dollars. Instead of throwing me out for not being old enough, they'd be begging for my business! I wondered how it would feel not having to worry about meeting payroll each week. Then there were all those people I owed money to, many of whom thought they owned me. I couldn't wait to be delivered from their clutches.

The only thing that remained after the prospectus was the legal documents. As president and chairman of the board, my signature was required on nearly every one. David Lundy handed me a stack of papers to sign. As I sat there and scanned the documents, I recalled what one of the lawyers had told me about lying to the Securities and Exchange Commission: "You'll go to jail for a long time if you defraud the SEC." His words haunted me. *It's not too late,* I thought. *I can stop the public offering now and minimize my potential punishment. Until this deal becomes effective and the stock is sold to the public, I'm not guilty of defrauding the SEC.*

It seemed like only days since my financial problems had been in the neighborhood of several hundred dollars instead of several million dollars. Time had simply added more zeros. I again looked down at the papers and feigned inspecting them. Sweat beaded up on my forehead. I glanced at my watch; it was 3:20 A.M. Defrauding thousands of people through a public stock offering was a lot different from stealing a few money orders or overcharging customer credit cards. *How did things get so out of hand?* I thought.

I had to have courage. This deal would supposedly make me the youngest person in history to take a company public on Wall Street, and I would raise fifteen million dollars. I was only *twenty years old!* Besides, I had people depending on me. Employees and investors needed to be paid. Stan was counting on me. And the ultimate goal was still the same—to keep ZZZZ Best running until January of 1988, when I would be home free!

I ran my fingers through my hair and rubbed my neck. The long day was catching up with me. I thought briefly about my friends at Cal State, Northridge, who lived free from stressful decisions in frat houses. But I had chosen a different route. I wanted the fame. I wanted the glory. I wanted everyone to know who Barry Minkow was. I wanted magazines, newspapers, and television shows singing the praises of the "Boy Genius."

I straightened the stack of legal documents on the table and grabbed my pen. I began signing. Page after page, signature after signature. The more I thought about the money, power, and glory, the faster I signed. At 3:55 A.M., my hand raced across the last page, and I handed the stack to David Lundy.

"Here you go, sir—signed, sealed, and delivered," I said with a smile.

David looked at me intently. "You should be proud of your accomplishments," he said. "It's not every day that a guy who is not even allowed to drink legally takes a company public." He offered his hand, but I hugged him instead.

If he only knew, I thought. *If he only knew.*

PART 3:
Collapse

Under Fire | 12

1 987 started off great. The fifteen-million-dollar public offering had sold out in December and funded. I had used the leverage from that to obtain additional bank loans—a total of $7 million. ZZZZ Best's stock value was pushing nearly fifty million, making my stock worth just shy of twenty-five million dollars.

On the advice of Howard Kane, I hired Thomas Meyer, a public relations man. Meyer was known for taking one small company's stock (it later became a large company) from two dollars to over two hundred dollars a share. Even Robert Fuller respected the way Meyer's firm was able to move stocks.

But I had trouble getting along with Meyer. He was just like me—he had to be in control. He criticized my staff and hurled insults at me on occasion. Many times I felt like telling him off, but I resisted the temptation because he was making me a hero on Wall Street. In just four months (January through April 1987), Meyer single-handedly took the stock from four dollars to over eighteen dollars a share, which put the company's stock value at just under three hundred million. My own stock was worth over one hundred million dollars!

As planned, I used some of the extra cash to do the TV ad campaign. The three commercials were humorous because they exposed how the competition often used "bait and switch" tactics on unsuspecting customers. These spots instantly became hits. I took great pleasure in starring in each of them, hoping to become so famous that I'd be noticed everywhere I went. It worked. By the end of February, I couldn't go anywhere in California without being recognized. Somehow that made the lying, manipulating, and conning a little easier to take.

With the company growing in popularity, we opened nine new locations between mid-December 1986 and mid-May 1987: three in Arizona, two in Nevada, and four in northern California. We even began to manufacture and private-label our own carpet-cleaning chemicals. All this pushed our employee total to well over twelve hundred company wide.

But the biggest news of 1987 was the KeyServ deal. I learned in early February that Northern Foods, a British company, wanted to sell one of its American subsidiaries, KeyServ, Inc. KeyServ was Sears Roebuck's authorized carpet cleaner, nationwide. When customers called Sears for carpet cleaning, KeyServ did the work. Sears got between 10 and 15 percent of the sale, with KeyServ retaining the balance. KeyServ's annual revenues topped eighty million dollars.

I saw acquiring KeyServ as a way to instantly fulfill my dream of becoming the *General Motors of the carpet-cleaning industry.* There were just two problems: the twenty-five-million-dollar price tag, and the fact that KeyServ was three times the size of ZZZZ Best, with almost three thousand employees.

When I brought the deal to Thomas Meyer, he assured me that he could raise the money for the acquisition. "I'll get your foot in the door with the investment bankers, but you have to sell them on the deal," Meyer told me.

I studied KeyServ's financial statements and business strategies, looking for areas needing improvement. I also flew to New Town Square, Pennsylvania, and met with the company's top management. That done, I was ready to sell the investment people.

At my first meeting with the corporate-finance people, I responded to every one of their concerns. If they had a question, I had a reasoned answer. Within hours they were satisfied enough to move forward. Truthfully, I think they were more persuaded by the dramatic increase in our stock price than by me. They were to receive a substantial portion of stock for funding the acquisition.

Carl Stowe and I viewed the KeyServ deal as the final link in the chain that would lead us to January of 1988. Since the investment banking firm was offering to raise an estimated $40 million we would use $25 million to buy out KeyServ and the balance to hold us over until January. We had soon figured out that the fifteen million dollars from the public offering and the $10 million in bank loans would still leave us cash short. The "profits" being paid to investors for the nonexistent restoration deals were depleting ZZZZ Best's cash surplus at an alarming rate.

As was the ad campaign. One of my advisors had hauled reams of computer printouts to my office in early March to deliver the news. "Mr. Minkow, these commercials are killing us!" he said.

"What do you mean?"

"Well, between the production costs and the air time, we've spent almost two million dollars."

"So?"

"The problem is, we've only taken in twenty thousand in business."

"How do you know that?"

"Because we used a special 800 number in the spots. The sales off that number only total twenty thousand dollars or so in business." He paused as I rubbed my cheek. "I think we should cancel all future television ads before we lose another two million."

He didn't understand. I didn't care about the cost-effectiveness of television advertising. I cared about every resident of California instantly recognizing my face.

"Don't cancel them," I said softly.

"What?" he asked in amazement.

"I said, *'Don't cancel them!'* It's called 'identity.' We're going to keep running these commercials until ZZZZ Best becomes a household name."

My advisor was astonished. He picked up his printouts and walked to the door. "Or until we go broke," he said before he left.

I chose not to respond.

❖ ❖ ❖

"Come on, Barry, you're going to be late for your own birthday party!" Donna called up the stairs.

I was upstairs getting dressed and could hear the flood of people coming through the door to celebrate my twenty-first birthday. I made my way down through streamers and balloons and all the trappings of a gala affair. Donna had done an outstanding job preparing the house for this, my very special day.

Though I hated turning twenty-one—I was now officially an adult and no longer legitimate heir to the titles "Boy Genius" or the "Whiz Kid of Wall Street"—I took comfort in my accomplishments. Twelve hundred employees, the fourth hottest stock on Wall Street, the KeyServ deal, and connections with powerful criminals who worked hard at keeping me alive. Yes, I had made a difference.

I stopped by the front door and greeted a few arriving guests. The place was jam-packed with people. Inside, there was standing room only, and outside, a line of people waited to get in.

"Did you invite the whole world to this party?" I asked Donna.

"No, Barry. Just your close friends and those who would be

offended if they weren't invited. . . . Just relax and have fun," she said as she kissed me on the cheek.

"I think for next year's party we're going to need a bigger house," I replied jokingly.

I turned around and bumped into Vera. "Look at this place, Barry," she said excitedly. "All these people love and care for you. . . . Isn't it great that they're here for you?"

"Yeah," I replied softly.

She gave me a big hug and went on her way. But what she said stuck with me. Did all these people really love me?

I made my way to the living room and found several of my top managers laughing and talking. They paused in their conversation and greeted me warmly. I thought about what Vera had said and then asked myself what they were doing here. *It's not because they love me, but because I sign their paychecks!* I said to myself. I faked a smile, shook a few hands, and strode into the family room, where Matt Paulson, David Lundy, and several of my financial advisors were yukking it up. *They're only here because of the hundreds of thousands of dollars I've paid in fees,* I thought. My frustration increased.

I threaded my way through the crowd and into the backyard where several of my investors were admiring my swimming pool with its tiled *Z* on the bottom. *I wish I had all the interest back that I've paid these people over the last two years,* I said to myself. *Do they like me for me, or for the "juice"?*

As I made my way back inside, I noticed Phil Cox hanging on the perimeter, watching my every move. When my gaze met Phil's, I thought about Robert and Stan. Just two weeks earlier, they had sold their half million shares of ZZZZ Best stock at eight dollars a share. I wondered why. The stock was going up and the KeyServ deal would close shortly, which was sure to push the stock up even further. *Do they know something they aren't telling me?* I suppressed the thought.

Finally, I went into the kitchen, hoping to find at least one person who honestly loved Barry Minkow because he was Barry Minkow. One of my best friends from high school was there talking with Donna. I looked closely at both of them, hoping to see two reasons for stifling my paranoia. But then I remembered the one thousand shares of ZZZZ Best stock I had bought for my friend just the week before. As I focused on Donna, I saw the five-thousand-dollar diamond ring she wore on her finger. Had I bought her too—maybe not intentionally, but . . . ?

A sick feeling came over me. Weak-kneed, I climbed the stairs to the peace and quiet of my bedroom—where I lay across the bed and cried.

❖ ❖ ❖

The shower jets struck my face forcefully as I struggled to wake up. It was Friday morning, May 22, 1987, and I was looking forward to a long Memorial Day weekend. *Maybe I'll drive the Testarossa to Palm Springs and just relax for three days,* I thought. I deserved a break after clocking fifteen-hour days putting together the KeyServ acquisition. By Tuesday, May 26, the deal would close, and I'd become the president and chairman of the board of the largest independently owned carpet-furniture-and drapery-cleaning company in the nation.

I rinsed the shampoo out of my hair and thought how great it was going to be to run a company with over three thousand employees. I fantasized about media interviews where I'd trumpet my success. I stepped out of the shower, excited and ready to take on the world. I glanced in the mirror to check out my physique. Though I'd tapered my workouts dramatically, the steroids had helped me retain most of my muscle mass.

Donna was still asleep, but as usual she had set out my clothes. I had no patience for coordinating clothing. I looked at the clock on the nightstand: it was 6:45 A.M. I pulled on my clothes and walked to the window. My English bulldog, Louy, was still fast asleep in his three-thousand-dollar doghouse in the backyard. *What a lazy dog!* I thought.

Seeing the *Z* at the bottom of the pool, sparkling in the morning sun, called up memories of the early days at ZZZZ Best. It seemed like only yesterday that I was struggling to come up with thirty-seven dollars for my first order of business cards. Now I was buying a nationally known company for twenty-five million dollars. I was proud of myself and enjoyed reflecting on my past accomplishments.

The phone wakened me from my dream world. *It's a little early for a phone call,* I thought. I picked up the receiver.

"Barry, is that you?" asked the voice on the other end of the line.

"Yeah, it's me. Who's this?"

"It's Thomas Meyer. Have you read your morning paper yet?"

Meyer had a house in a posh L.A. suburb and often flew out from back east for extended periods. For him to call me at home this early it had to be serious.

"No, I haven't," I responded. "Should I?"

"Yeah! The article we feared that reporter would write made the front page of today's metro section."

"How bad is it, Thomas?"

"It's pretty bad, Barry. It talks about your past involvement with credit card fraud. Your stock is already down half a point. When are you going to be at the office?"

"I'm on my way."

"Good. I'll call you in half an hour. We're going to need to prepare some kind of press release to explain this thing away." He hung up the phone.

So much for an easy day. I rushed down the stairs and out to the porch where I stooped to grab the *L.A. Times.* My heart rate increased as I pulled out the business section. There it was: my picture in the top right-hand corner next to a bold-print headline: **"Behind Whiz Kid Lies Trail of False Credit Card Billings."** A cold chill ran down my spine.

There was no time to stand there and read the article. I had to get to the office—fast. I roared out of the driveway and got on the phone to John Brady, the stockbroker who had been introduced to me by Robert Fuller. He monitored ZZZZ Best's stock and alerted me to every significant change.

"John, it's Barry. Is everything all right?"

"I just tried to call you at the office. Have you read the article yet?" His voice betrayed him. He was almost panic-stricken.

"I've got it right here in front of me. It's old news, John. Nothing to be concerned about," I said in a convincing tone.

"I hope you're right, Barry. The stock is down seven-eighths."

"Listen, John, we're going to be preparing a press release to respond to this article, so don't worry."

"But, Barry, I've already had two clients call with sell orders," he argued. "They read the article and called me immediately."

"Well, why didn't you stick up for me and assure them that nothing was wrong with the company?" I yelled into the receiver.

"Take it easy, pal. I didn't know *what* to say."

"If any other stockholders call and want to sell, let them know you talked to me and I said everything was okay. Emphasize the fact that this credit card nonsense is *three years old!* Have you got that?"

"Yeah," he answered in a dejected tone.

I sensed his disappointment. "Listen, I've never let you down since I've known you, and I'm not about to start now! I've told you this thing ain't nothing. I'll have it all worked out within a couple of days. In the meantime, do your best to prevent people from dumping the stock, okay?"

By the time our conversation ended, I was within five minutes of the office. *Why did this thing have to break four days before I close the biggest deal of my life?* I asked myself. I was panicking. I pulled into the parking lot and rushed to my office. It was only 7:15, and the phone was already ringing off the hook.

I picked up the phone on the fourth ring. "This is Barry Minkow."

"Thomas Meyer, Barry. Listen, I'm going to set up a conference call with a few brokers from New York. They have some questions they want answered about the article. I think it's important for *you* to speak with them before this thing gets out of hand."

"I agree. What time do you want to do it?"

"Now!"

"All right. But I just got in, and there's no one here to answer the phones, so we might be interrupted," I explained.

"That's fine. I'll get us cross-connected. Just hold on."

As I waited, I read the article from start to finish. It was damaging because it alleged *patterns* of criminal behavior and denial. But it didn't mention the phony restoration business. *As long as that isn't discovered, I can overcome all this other stuff,* I decided.

"Barry, it's me. . . . Are you ready?" Thomas asked when he came back on the line.

"Sure, Thomas. Put them on," I said with a sudden burst of confidence.

"Barry, this is Byron Buckley from Johnston & Lang. I've got a couple of associates on the line with me, and we just want to ask you a few questions. Is that okay?" I had met Buckley a few months earlier. He ran the Los Angeles office of Johnston & Lang, and had been very enthusiastic about ZZZZ Best stock.

"Go right ahead, gentlemen. Ask away."

"Has anyone from your investment banking firm called you yet to cancel the forty-million-dollar funding for the acquisition?" asked Buckley.

"No, sir. I haven't heard anything from our people, and I don't expect to. I informed them weeks ago that a negative article might come out about some past credit-card overcharges, and they didn't seem concerned. I would be very surprised if they reacted at all to this outdated news story."

"Well, are you going to prepare a press release of some kind to neutralize this article? There's a lot of selling pressure on the stock right now."

"Mr. Meyer and I were discussing that earlier," I answered. "We'll make a public statement that will explain the entire situation and put this whole credit card issue to rest."

"What actually happened, Barry?" asked Buckley. "I mean, how were all these customers overcharged?"

Telling Byron Buckley the truth was not an option. "I had some dishonest carpet cleaners who worked for the company a while back who overcharged customers to increase their commissions," I lied. "When I found out about the scheme, I fired them and paid back all the victims. What more could I do?"

"I understand what you're saying and I believe you," said Buckley. "If I didn't, I wouldn't be talking to you now. But the public isn't aware yet of *your side* of the story, and we need to make them aware as soon as possible."

"I plan on doing that today, sir."

"Good. Meanwhile, let me know if you hear from your investors. The best thing you can do right now is close that financing deal. That would immediately silence the critics and stop the selling."

"That sounds great to me, Mr. Buckley," I replied. "I'll do whatever I can to get it done."

"Keep us posted and I'll call you later."

"How's the stock now?" I asked before he hung up.

"It's down one and a half," he answered. The conversation ended.

I sat back and massaged my temples, feeling a bad headache coming on. There had to be a way for me to stop the free-fall. For every point my stock dropped, I personally lost six million dollars in net worth.

The intercom buzzed. It was Amy—in early as usual. She was typically solicitous. "Are you all right?"

"I've been better. You know about the article, I suppose?"

"Yeah, but don't worry, Barry, everything will be okay! I've got faith in you!" she said in a kindly voice. "Can I bring you some coffee?"

"Sure, and bring two aspirin with you. Also, because of this article, the phone's going to be ringing off the hook today, so just put the calls through as fast as you can. It's called 'damage control,'" I said.

"No problem. I'll be in there in a few minutes."

The phone buzzed again. *More good news,* I thought to myself.

"Sorry to bother you again," Amy said, "but Miles Harris from the investment banking firm is on the line. He says it's important. Do you want to talk to him?"

Only two weeks before, Harris had been generous with praise at the convention, which had brought the KeyServ and ZZZZ Best management teams together. Now I feared even taking his call.

"Put him through, Amy," I said, then addressed the caller with forced enthusiasm, "Hi, Miles. How are you?"

"Not good, Barry. I'm sure you're aware of this morning's *L.A. Times* article?"

"Of course I am, Miles. I told you this story might come out sooner or later. The contents don't surprise me in the least," I lied. I had disclosed the likelihood of some negative publicity, but I had played it very low-key. Naively, I suppose, I hadn't expected the story to be so bold and hard-hitting, nor to be given front-page metro status—with my photo, no less.

"Well, Barry, the story concerns me and a few of our top executives. Before we close the forty-million-dollar funding, we want to reinvestigate this entire credit card deal."

"But that stuff's three years old, Miles," I objected.

"Since it's our money, we'll be the judge of what's relevant to investigate," he snapped. "I want to fly in our investigators immediately. They'll spend the weekend with you and ask detailed questions about the contents of the article. If your answers can be independently verified, everything should be okay. If not, we'll back out of the deal immediately."

The article had put a lot of heat on Miles. He was supposed to know things like this and have answers prepared. But the news had caught him off guard. Now he was professionally embarrassed and determined to get to the bottom of this alleged credit card fraud.

"That's fine with me. I'll spend the three-day weekend answering questions. Whatever information they need, I'll provide," I said. Amy slid the coffee in front of me. I took the aspirin and hoped that it would work quickly.

"Good," Miles replied. "I'll set everything up and have the investigators meet you at your office between eight and eight-thirty tomorrow morning."

"Are you guys going to say anything to the press?"

"We have nothing to say at this point. Right now we need to concentrate on completing the investigation," Miles replied.

"I'll be waiting for them tomorrow morning."

There goes the relaxing weekend, I thought, as I hung up the phone. This investigation worried me. Until this article, no one had been *looking* for fraud at ZZZZ Best. I was the whiz-kid entrepreneur underdog who had overcome youth and built an empire. But now, the authenticity of the Barry Minkow story was in doubt. These investigators would come looking for impropriety, and that kind of scrutiny terrified me.

I knew I should inform Byron Buckley about the call from Miles. But if I did, he might turn sour on ZZZZ Best. That phone call would have to wait. I glanced at my watch. *I've already been through an entire day of aggravation, and it's not even eight o'clock,* I thought.

"Barry," I heard Amy say on the intercom, "Channel 2 News

is on the line. They want to know if they can come out and do an interview with you. What should I tell them?''

I mentally reviewed my options. *Maybe I can use this free air time to defend my integrity,* I reasoned. For years I had used the media to convince the public that ZZZZ Best was legitimate. Now I needed to attack the critics head-on and systematically answer their questions. *By creating a stage and putting on a performance (like I did only weeks ago at the convention), I can get out of this mess too,* I thought.

"Ask them if they can be here before two o'clock, Amy."

Within minutes, she had confirmed a one-thirty interview time.

"That's great!" I responded. "If any other media people call, tell them I'll make a formal statement here in my office at that time."

"All right," said Amy. "Can I come and straighten your desk before they get here?"

I smiled. The desk was nearly invisible beneath mounds of paper—not a good impression for the evening news. Amy always thought of that sort of thing. "Sure," I replied. "Come in around twelve-thirty."

My attitude suddenly took a 180-degree turn. My television presence had never failed me in the past, and I felt confident that I could neutralize this story before it really blew up. I walked to the window and peeked through the blinds at my employees, answering phones and setting up carpet-cleaning appointments. *These people work for me!* I thought proudly. *And there's no way I'm going to let them down!*

"Barry?" I heard Amy's faint voice and ran over to pick up the receiver. "It's Stan. . . . He says it's urgent."

Into the Abyss | 13

S tan, how are you?" I said cheerfully.

"Well, it's the wonder boy," he joked. "How are you, whiz?"

"I've had better days," I replied. "I'm sure you're aware of the problems I'm having with the media."

"As a matter of fact, I am. Do you think it would be possible to get fifteen minutes of your time today, Mr. Wonder Boy?" It was unusual for Stan to call me directly—normally Robert or Phil was the message bearer—and more unusual that he wanted to see me on such short notice. I concluded that it must be serious.

"Of course I can spare fifteen minutes for you. What time do you want to see me?"

"How does now sound?" His voice had lost its humorous tone.

"Now, Stan?" I was caught off guard. "Can I make it later on this afternoon? I don't mean to put you off, but I've got a lot going on with this article, and I need to be here for a few hours. How about four o'clock?" I asked tentatively. Stan did not like to be put off.

"If that's as soon as you can make it, I'll see you then."

"Great! I'll see you no later than four today. How are you feeling? . . ."

There was no answer. He had hung up.

I stood and paced the office nervously. *Why is Stan so anxious to see me?* I asked myself. The last thing I needed was a problem with him. *I warned him about that newspaper story two weeks ago, knowing how he hates to be surprised.*

Just then Amy chimed in on the intercom, "It's the branch manager from Citizens Credit—"

"Put him through," I interrupted. Citizens Credit was where I had my main business checking account. I owed the bank $3 million and planned to pay it back when the merger financing was completed.

"Hello, how are you this morning?" I asked cordially.

"I'm doing fine, Barry. But I think we have a small problem."

Problem was not a word I enjoyed hearing from my banker. "What might that be, sir?" I asked respectfully.

"I'm going to have to call your loan, Barry. I hate to do that, but based on the information in today's paper, the bank is quite concerned about ZZZZ Best's credibility."

My head spun. *One lousy article and the bank's going to jump ship on me,* I thought. *What fair-weather friends they turned out to be.* "Sir, I think there's a big misunderstanding about this article. This whole credit card thing is old news and has nothing to do with our current operations," I protested.

"I'm sure that's true, Barry. And after the loan is paid back, we can go over it in more detail. But for now, the bank would feel more comfortable if the loan were paid in full. According to our agreement, the bank has the option to levy your checking account to pay the loan."

"You can't levy my checking account! All my company checks will bounce! I'll be out of business!" I yelled as I jumped out of my chair.

"Relax. I didn't say we've decided to do that today, Barry. I'm merely stating that we have that option. But I would like to see a significant reduction within five days, or I will levy the account to protect the bank's interest."

This was devastating news. I couldn't pay back Citizens

Credit unless the investment money came through. And since the investment firm had just delayed the deal, I was in real trouble. But I couldn't let the bank know this.

"That's fair enough. Give me five days, and I'll make a major reduction in the loan." I paused to let the offer sink in. "By the way, tonight on Channel 2 News, you'll see my official reply to today's article. I would appreciate your watching the program."

"I'll do that, and I'll get some of my associates to do the same. Perhaps you can earn back some credibility with a strong explanation."

"You can bet I will," I responded. "And have a nice weekend."

I hung up the phone and called the only person who could help in this situation—Carl Stowe. I wasn't about to take on the world single-handedly any longer. "Carl, it's Barry. I need to see you right away."

"What's wrong, partner? Is everything all right?" Carl was a late riser and had not yet seen the article.

I filled him in on my day so far—the *Times* story, the plummeting stock, the investors, Citizens Credit.

"Was there anything in the article about the restoration business?" he asked.

"No, Carl, and that's what amazes me. They don't have a clue as to what's *really* going on, yet everyone's still jumping ship. But don't worry. I'm going on television in a few hours, and then I'll publicly put this thing to rest."

"I'm on my way. What's the stock trading at now?"

"The last I heard, it was down a point and a half."

"Don't worry, Barry. We'll handle this problem and close the investment deal. We've done it before when the chips were down, and we can do it again."

My phone was blinking, indicating another incoming call. "You're right, pal! See you in a few."

I quickly hung up and asked Amy who it was. I glanced at my watch . . . 10:00 A.M. This was turning out to be the longest day of my life.

"It's John Brady, Barry. He says it's important."

"Put him through." I wondered if I'd ever receive another call that *wasn't* important. "Yes, John, what's going on with the stock?"

"Everything bad," he said over the background clatter of a brokerage office on a trading day. "Unless you're on the short side. It's down two and three-quarters, and there's a ton of selling pressure. You have any idea who's doing all this selling?"

I tried to brighten John's mood by telling him how my upcoming press conference would take head-on the issue of the old credit card billing story.

"That should slow the selling," I said. "You can count on me, John. I'll call you later."

As the conversation ended, I remembered the time John and I had gone to a ball game together. We'd had a great time—laughing, joking. John had believed in me and ZZZZ Best. *What will happen to him if this all falls apart? The whole thing has gotten totally out of hand,* I thought.

The intercom buzzed again.

"Barry, Rhonda Ames from Western Hills Savings and Loan is on the line," Amy said.

"I'm falling in love with today. . . . Put her through." I owed Western Hills $7 million. "Hi, Rhonda. How are you?" I asked when she came on the line.

"That's a question I should be asking you, Barry. Is everything all right over there?" she asked.

"Of course it is," I lied. "Just a little bad press—nothing I can't handle. I'll be holding a press conference later when I'll explain everything."

"I've noticed your stock is down quite a bit today. Have you heard from the investment people?"

"No, I haven't. They were prepared for this article because I disclosed the problem to them weeks ago." The lies just rolled off my tongue.

She changed the subject. "When are you going to be able to pay the loan back?"

The last thing I needed was another five-day mandatory pay-down. "I'd say within the next thirty to forty-five days, I should be able to clear the debt."

"Can't you do it any sooner?"

"Well, Rhonda, I have over twelve hundred employees to pay every week, not to mention my normal expenses. I planned on paying you back in late June when I'm in a better cash position."

"Yeah, but with this latest article, my boss is a little concerned. He wants the loan paid now, and by our loan agreement we have the right to demand that the note be paid at any time!" she insisted.

I was getting an education in finance. Whenever a bank got a little nervous, it had the right to call a loan. Somehow that rule didn't seem fair, but I was in no position to argue.

"I'll tell you what I can do, Rhonda. Why don't you fax me a personal guarantee letter for the loan, and I'll sign it and return it to you immediately. That way, you not only have ZZZZ Best's guarantee, but you also have my personal guarantee. And since I'm worth over one hundred million, that should increase your comfort level."

"I'm glad you suggested that, because that's one of the reasons I called. The bank definitely wants your personal guarantee on this loan. Also, I think you should be aware that we've frozen the funds in your business checking account."

"You did *what?*" I yelled. "Did you bounce my company checks?"

"No, but I'd suggest you not write any more checks against the account," she said.

I didn't push the issue. Only a $7-million cashier's check

made out to Western Hills would change her mind. "If that's the way you want it, I'll stop writing checks on the account."

"Good. And I'll fax the personal guarantee form as soon as I hang up. I'll also tell my superiors that the loan will be paid in full within thirty days."

"No problem, Rhonda."

I slowly put down the receiver and rested my head in my hands. With my cash at Western Hills tied up, I didn't have enough money to meet next week's payroll. *Where in the world is Carl?* I thought. I grabbed the phone.

"Amy! Where is Carl? He was supposed to be here an hour ago!" I snapped.

"He called and said he had to go to the bank and then see one of the investors. He forgot to tell you that when you called." She sensed my disappointment. "I would have told you sooner, but you've been on the phone."

"That's okay, Amy. . . . By the way, Western Hills will be faxing a document for me to sign. Just bring it in when it arrives."

"I'll be looking for it," she said. "Want me to pick you up some lunch?"

"No, I'm not hungry, but thanks for offering."

I looked at my watch—11:17 A.M. In less than five hours' time, my world had crashed: The banks had called their loans, the investment firm had postponed the deal pending an investigation I was sure to fail, Stan wanted to see me (it couldn't be good news), I was out of cash, and my stock was dropping as each minute passed.

Amy walked in with the fax. "That was quick," I commented. "These people must be worried." I signed the form. "Go ahead and fax it back to them and mail the hard copy to Rhonda Ames's attention."

"Yes, sir," she replied. "Barry, I know you're swamped, but there's a managers' meeting going on downstairs in the conference room. I really think you need to make an appearance to pick up the morale."

"Who's going to pick up mine?" I quipped. But she was right. "All right, Amy, I'll be there in a minute."

I walked out of the office, down the stairs, and into the conference room. Mike McGee was addressing the store managers in the mandatory, biweekly staff meeting. His tone was troubled, the atmosphere in the room, subdued. I walked to the front, hoping to bring enthusiasm and encouragement to a dejected management team.

"Good afternoon, ladies and gentlemen," I greeted them cordially. "I realize that the article in today's *L.A. Times* has caused some concern. But I don't want you to allow it to affect the morale of this company. Mr. McGee has been with me for almost five years and can testify that we have continually overcome every obstacle that has been set in our path. This will be no different." I walked back and forth, trying to generate some momentum. "People are jealous of a winner—and that's why they want to see us fail! But nothing's changed on our agenda. We're still going to become the biggest carpet-and-furniture-cleaning company in the United States!"

But even *I* wasn't convinced. My delivery lacked its usual confidence and buoyancy. Too many things going on. I noticed Amy motioning me from the back of the room. The press was early.

"Unfortunately, I have to cut this short, but I want all of you to continue as if this article never appeared. 'Business as usual' will be our motto." With that, I strode off, to an audience reaction singular in my career as a public speaker—dead silence.

In my absence, a dozen or so reporters, cameramen, and radio people had swarmed into my office. Lights were glaring, cameras were mounted, tape recorders were readied, notebooks were poised. And I was worried. *If I couldn't convince my own sympathetic audience, how am I going to persuade a hostile one?*

"We're ready, Mr. Minkow, if you are," came a voice from the crowd.

I pulled my chair into the well of my desk, ran a comb through my hair, and straightened my back. The pressure was on and my fate was in my own hands—just as I wanted it to be. "I'm ready."

"Four, three, two, one . . . Mr. Minkow, can you comment on why your stock went down four points today?"

The question startled me. I didn't know the stock had dropped *that* much—I had personally taken a twenty-four-million-dollar hit. My knees went weak.

"I believe the drop in our stock can be attributed to an article in the *L.A. Times* that described a past problem we encountered with some dishonest carpet cleaners. They had overcharged some customers, and when I found out about it, they were subsequently fired. There really isn't much more to it," I said, trying to minimize the offense.

"Is it true that the Securities and Exchange Commission has ordered a formal investigation of ZZZZ Best?"

Again I was caught off guard. This was the first I'd heard of any SEC investigation. I hated being on the defensive. In past television interviews, I had been in charge and had dictated the pace. "I'm not aware of any such investigation."

Before I could expound further, another reporter waved a copy of our company prospectus in the air. "Mr. Minkow, in your prospectus it states that you completed a seven-million-dollar restoration project in Sacramento. But when I checked to see if ZZZZ Best had filed any permits for such construction, none were found. In fact, ZZZZ Best doesn't even possess a contractor's license. Can you explain this?"

The minute I heard the phrase "restoration projects," I knew my days were numbered. They were on to me. *How in the world did they connect my past credit card fraud with the restoration business?* I asked myself.

But I couldn't leave the question unanswered. "I'm going to have to refer that question to our legal staff. They are better equipped to answer that. I've got time for one more question," I said, trying to cut my losses—but I was really only fueling the fire.

"Is it true that your investors have backed out of the financing for the acquisition?" someone asked.

"That's false!" I snapped. "They have done no such thing. . . . That's all for today."

I walked briskly out of the office and stopped at Amy's desk. "I'll be back in an hour," I told her. She knew intuitively that I was in big trouble.

I got in my car and sped to Stan's condominium. I glanced at my watch—it was only 1:15 P.M. *Will this day never end?* I thought.

As I drove, I attempted to systematize my many problems. I had overcome insurmountable odds before, but this challenge was clearly the most difficult. I took a deep breath and cranked the stereo—that had worked in the past. I was no quitter, but in my heart of hearts, I knew it was only a matter of time before my empire collapsed. My eyes started to water. The thought of failure scared me more than anything else. I longed to be shaken from this bad dream and told that everything was all right. Smiling people walked along the street, happy kids played in the yards. I wished I were they. No, I wished I were anyone but me.

I parked in back of Stan's condo and walked through the door. "Stan!" I called loudly. "Are you there?" I was one of the privileged few who didn't have to knock.

"Come on in, Wonder Boy," said the joking voice. "I'm in the kitchen."

I walked in, gave him the ritual kiss on the cheek, and sat down. *Here I am, barely twenty-one years old, and kissing gangster types as if I've known them for years. How did I get myself into this mess?* I asked myself.

Stan stared at me. "You look terrible, kid."

"You're one to talk," I said jokingly. Stan was wearing his

"uniform"—pants with no shirt—and was smoking a cigarette. "I've had a hard day," I continued. "No . . . let me rephrase that. I've had the *worst* day of my life!"

Stan smiled and smoked, staring at me the same way he'd stared at Charlie Hunter that day in the limousine. I was nervous.

"You can't be mad at me over this article, Stan," I protested. "I warned you about it the minute the reporter started calling and asking questions three weeks ago."

"What I have to talk to you about has nothing to do with the article," he replied. "I called you here to tell you a few things I didn't want to say over the phone." He put his cigarette in the ashtray. "You're being investigated by the L.A. Police Department."

"I'm *what?*"

"I didn't stutter, kid. ZZZZ Best, and you specifically, are the target of a major investigation," he said in a serious tone.

I put my head in my hands. "What else can go wrong?" I replied in disbelief.

"I'm telling you so you can watch your back and be careful what you say over the phone . . . which leads me to my next point. . . ."

"More good news, I suppose?" I said sarcastically.

Stan got up, walked to the sink, and filled a glass with water. He drank it slowly before proceeding. "You've got a leak in your ranks, kid."

"What's that supposed to mean?" I snapped.

"What that means," he said, "is that someone from within your ranks is spilling their guts about what's going on at ZZZZ Best." He walked back to the table and sat down. "So far, this individual has told certain people that the Sacramento restoration job was a fraud."

"Who's the leak, Stan?" I demanded.

"We don't know yet, but when I find out, I'll tell you. I warned you time and again about those bozos who hang around you."

Stan had never liked Carl Stowe, because he knew Ron Knox

had introduced us. He also didn't seem to care for others I associated with.

"What do you want me to do, Stan?" I asked softly.

"There's nothing you can do, kid. Much of the damage has already been done. It's only a matter of time before they bury you. I'm giving you the freedom to do whatever you want to try to save the company." He picked up his cigarette. "But, in my opinion, it's too late."

"Are you going to pull your people out of the stock?" I asked. I knew the answer.

"What do you think?"

"I think that I don't have a fighting chance." I wanted to leave, but I had one more question. "Is that why you sold out early, Stan?" My question sparked his interest. "Did you know then that it was only a matter of months before I fell?" I waited for his reply, but he said nothing. "I've got to get back to the office." I got up, gave him a quick kiss on the cheek out of respect, and walked to the door.

Fighting back tears, I called Amy on my way back to the office to check on my phone messages. "Hi, Amy, it's Barry."

"I'm glad you called. The phone has been ringing off the hook. Everybody is yelling and demanding that you call them right away."

I passed a playground and saw little children playing baseball. I thought back to my Little League days and wished I could relive them. ZZZZ Best—the company that I had fought so hard to build—was crumbling. I pictured the failed interview with the press. They knew about the phony restoration business. I recalled Stan's words about the leak.

"Who called?" I struggled to ask.

"Rhonda Ames, Miles Harris, Citizens Credit, John Brady, Thomas Meyer, Byron Buckley, Robert Fuller . . ." The phone clattered to the floorboard.

I pulled over and cried—and then I thought about suicide.

Forty-Two Days | 14

I picked up the phone and called Amy back to tell her I'd be there in fifteen minutes. My vision was blurred with tears, so I remained at the side of the highway.

The phone rang again. *Now who?* I thought as I picked up the receiver.

"Barry, it's Sheri. How are you?" It was my sister.

"Well, honey, I'm struggling. How are you?" The traffic raced by. I looked out the window; no one seemed to care that my life was unraveling. Maybe Sheri would.

"I read the article in the paper and talked to Mom. She said the stock was down almost four and a half points! Are you okay?"

"I don't know, honey. I'm trying to hold things together, but everybody seems to want to jump ship."

"I won't, Barry! I love you and I'm behind you all the way. You've made it through tough situations before, and you can do it again!" she said with confidence.

Her simple words of encouragement strengthened me. Maybe there was a way out. I *had* made it through difficult times before and had always come out on top. Maybe this temporary setback could be turned into another Barry Minkow "victory." I couldn't just give up. I had to try. There was too much at stake.

"Listen," she went on, "I'm going to Europe for two months with a friend. But I'll be pulling for you. Hang in there and don't let this thing get you down."

I sat up straighter and put my favorite cassette into the tape deck—"The Eye of the Tiger," theme song from *Rocky III*. But before I cranked up the volume, I had to say good-bye to my sister. "You'll never know how much this call means to me, Sheri. I'll love you forever, and I'll be thinking of you while you're away."

"I'll miss you too. . . . Now go get 'em!"

As I turned up the stereo, I looked in the mirror and wiped away the tears. The music shot bolts of energy through my veins as I headed for ZZZZ Best headquarters. *It ain't over 'til it's over!* I said to myself.

❖ ❖ ❖

"Amy, hold my calls. I need to coach Mike about the investigators."

"Okay, Barry, but can I go home now? It's almost seven."

"Sure you can. And thanks for helping me through this nightmare of a day."

"Anything for you, Barry. Make sure you get something to eat. I'm worried about your health."

"Yes, Mother," I joked. She left.

"Okay, Mike, here's the deal. The investigators from Washington will be here tomorrow morning and they're staying all weekend, including Monday." He was listening attentively. Mike was scared. He wasn't used to high-pressure situations.

"They'll ask both of us questions about the credit card fraud, and our answers have got to be consistent," I said, pacing back and forth.

"But I don't know anything about the overcharges, Barry. What am I going to say?" he asked nervously.

"Well, I want you to tell them that we had a group of carpet cleaners we hired from another company who worked for us as subcontractors. Because they were paid on commission, they inflated some of their sales by increasing the dollar amounts on the credit card slips. When we found out about the overcharges, we fired the people involved and paid back all the customers." Mike was resting his head in his hands. "That's the story. I want to keep it simple."

"What if they ask for names?"

"Good question. Tell them the incident happened so long ago that you'll have to check the files. By then I'll have thought of something."

"So we're going to lie to these people, Barry?"

"Yeah, we're going to lie to them! This stupid credit card thing is almost three years old, and nobody lost any money because of it," I said sternly.

"But these guys are trained investigators. They'll catch us. I don't think it's a good idea."

I stomped over to his chair and got in his face. "Listen to me, Mike, and listen good! When you came to me you had nothing! I'm the one who brought you two new cars and a new house. I'm the one who gave you a great job with this company! And if I say *lie*, you're gonna lie! Do you understand me?" I didn't often yell at Mike, but too much was riding on this investigation.

"Very good, Mr. Minkow," he said dejectedly. "I'll do exactly what you say."

"Good. I'll see you here tomorrow morning at eight o'clock." He left the office.

❖ ❖ ❖

"It's the smartest thing you can do, Barry. It shows the investment community that you've got nothing to hide," Thomas Meyer said.

"What's the name of the firm you want for the independent investigation?" I asked as I yawned into my bedroom phone. It was now 9:30 P.M. on this, the longest day of my life. I didn't feel up to arguing about retaining a law firm to conduct an independent investigation of the allegations made against the company.

Thomas gave me the name of a prominent L.A. firm. "I'll arrange everything over the weekend, and they'll start work on Tuesday morning," he said.

"How am I supposed to deal with the investigators for the investment firm and these lawyers at the same time?" I asked.

"I'm not talking about a long, drawn-out process. Both of these investigations shouldn't take more than two to four weeks."

"But I've got a company to run, Mr. Meyer. I can't spend the next four weeks talking to a bunch of stuffed-shirt lawyers."

"If you want to save your company, you'd better *find* the time!" he answered.

"All right," I said reluctantly. "I'll get it done."

After hanging up, I got into bed and rethought the events of the day. *Maybe I can skate through these investigations and close the KeyServ deal,* I thought. But then I remembered Stan's words: "You've got a leak, kid." Who was this leak, and how did he know that the Sacramento restoration job was a fraud? I had to find out more.

Then there were the banks. They were scared and wanted their money. I couldn't deposit any new funds into either Western Hills or Citizens Credit, because they'd use the money to offset my loans. But I had all kinds of expenses and the employee payrolls, which had to be paid with checks. I'd have to open a checking account at a new bank. And I'd have to come up with some money to put into that checking account, just to keep things going. Our funding had been postponed; I'd already reborrowed from Paul and Lee. Where could I get some big money fast?

Pat Chapman came to mind. As the successful owner of a manufacturing company, he admired my ambition and had offered to help me any way he could, even to loan money to the company. We had met several years earlier and had immediately hit it off. *He's good for at least a million,* I thought. I was sure he would help.

The second source I thought of was at the investment firm in New York. The company had lent me $5 million against some of my restricted ZZZZ Best stock. Unfortunately, I could only use these funds to buy securities through a stock-trading account I had set up at the company. But I had a hunch that my account representative there might approve a $1- or $2-million cash advance against the account. Between Chapman and the New York investment firm, I could feasibly raise enough money to survive until the investigations were over.

I closed my eyes that night, determined not to give up without a fight.

❖   ❖   ❖

"Mr. Minkow, we're going to want to interview you and Mr. McGee separately," said the investigator from the investment firm.

I nodded. "That's fine with me, sir. You can meet with me first, and then with Mr. McGee. Is that okay with you?"

"Yes, but before we begin, I'll need all the documents relating to the credit card fraud, including the names and addresses of the men responsible for the crime."

I reached into a desk drawer, pulled out a thick file, and casually handed it to the investigator, trying not to look as if I were holding anything back. "This is all the information I have. The customer invoices and proof of their repayment are included," I told him.

"What about the names of those responsible?" he pressed.

"Well, sir, since it all happened almost three years ago, I'll have to dig that up for you. I don't have it offhand."

He looked at me intently and then briefly reviewed the contents of the folder. "Before I can complete my investigation, I'm going to need those names, but I suppose this is enough to get started."

❖ ❖ ❖

"It went well," I said to Thomas Meyer. "They asked me questions on the credit card fraud for three hours, and I answered every one of them. I even gave them a tour of the facility and showed them the systems I've installed to prevent such a thing from happening again. Now they're talking to Mike."

"Good," he said. "I've talked to the law firm, and they're ready to begin. Two of their men will be at your office at nine o'clock Tuesday morning. Are you completing all your restoration work on time?"

"Yeah," I lied. "We're right on schedule. Why do you ask?"

"Because we're going to prepare a press release so the company can officially respond to all the allegations made in the article. I also want to include some positive information about the restoration business. It'll definitely help the stock."

"Sounds good to me, Mr. Meyer," I said excitedly.

"Call me later."

I hung up and enjoyed a few moments of peace and quiet. With the stock market and banks closed, the office phone lines were silent. Then I set out to raise some money. I called my contact at the New York investment firm at a private number, and talked him into a two-million-dollar bridge loan.

"Don't let me down, Barry," he warned. "I've got to have that money back in four weeks."

I assured him he'd have it, and called Pat Chapman and arranged to meet with him the following morning. Then the phone rang.

"Barry, is that you?" It was Gary.

"Yeah, pal. How's it going?"

"Not good, Barry. I've got to see you right away." It wasn't like Gary to demand a meeting on such short notice.

"Is there a problem?"

"A big one. But I can't talk about it over the phone."

"All right. I'll meet you at the Derrick's Diner in ten minutes."

Before I left, I looked down toward Mike's office and saw that he was still with the investigators. *Hope that's going well,* I fretted.

As I drove down Reseda Boulevard, I tried to think of what could possibly have gone wrong with Gary and Reliable Appraisal Company. Had the media called him? Was he having financial problems? *Just when I think things are beginning to work out, another crisis comes along!* I slammed my hands against the steering wheel.

Gary arrived five minutes after I did. He looked worried.

"You look like you haven't slept for a week," I said. "What's wrong?"

"Thanks a lot!" he snapped. "You don't look much better."

"So what's the big news, Gary? You're making me crazy trying to figure it out."

"Do you remember a man by the name of Paul Dennis?"

"Yeah, he was that guy who did some part-time work for you. What about him?"

"Well, it seems that he went to your accounting firm and told them that the Sacramento restoration job was a fraud."

"What!" I yelled. "How on earth does he know anything about our restoration business?"

"I don't know for sure. I think he overheard you and me talking on the phone and just put two and two together."

I frowned, then slammed my fist on the table.

"Don't worry, man. I know it looks bad, but we can still make it," Gary said.

I resisted the temptation to yell at him for allowing Dennis to learn about the restoration business.

❖　❖　❖

So that's the big leak Stan warned me about, I said to myself as I drove to see Pat Chapman early the next morning. I had tossed and turned most of the night, trying to figure out how to salvage the company's relationship with the high-powered accounting firm. If they were to resign based on what Dennis had told them, the press would jump all over the fact that our accounting firm had quit, and they'd force me to further substantiate the restoration business, which I couldn't do. Although I knew Meyer, Lundy, and others involved with ZZZZ Best would soon find out about the Dennis allegations, I decided not to tell them. *It's important that I look as surprised as they do when the news hits,* I thought as I pulled into Pat's driveway.

After a warm greeting and a brief tour of the house, we sat down in his dining room. "I hate to bother you on a holiday weekend, Pat, but it's really important," I began.

"No problem, Barry. Anything for you," Pat replied happily.

"I appreciate that." I felt uncomfortable about asking him for so much money. Even though I'd raised millions of dollars over the past three years, this time it was different. Maybe it was because I was there in Pat's home. Or maybe it was because I liked him so much. Lying to potential investors had become second-nature to me. But then I realized what was bothering me: In the past I'd always borrowed, knowing I could eventually pay the money back. This time I wasn't so sure. Deep down, I knew that if the investigations turned out badly, or if the accounting firm confirmed Dennis' story, I'd be through, and Pat would lose his money.

Nonetheless, I set those feelings aside and did what I did best—lie!

"Pat, I need to borrow at least a million dollars short-term, so I can complete a few of the restoration jobs. Two of the banks called their loans Friday, and that's put me in a real bind. I need your help, and I'm willing to give you my house as collateral."

"That's a lot of money, Barry. It's going to take me a week or so to raise that much. Can you wait that long?"

I nodded, relieved that he seemed so willing to help me with no questions asked. "Sure. If that's what it takes, I can manage 'til then."

"Good, then I'll get my lawyer on it right away. He'll want you to sign a few documents, but that shouldn't delay things. Is that okay with you?"

"It sure is, Pat. And I really appreciate your help." I walked over to his chair and shook his hand.

"There are not too many people I'd lend that kind of money to on such short notice, but I trust you, Barry, and I'm happy to help."

I couldn't look him in the eye.

❖ ❖ ❖

"What's the stock trading at now?" I asked John Brady from my car phone on Tuesday morning.

"It's down almost a point, and there's a lot of selling pressure on it. It's about to go below ten dollars a share," he said.

"Relax, John. We'll be making an announcement Thursday morning that'll help bring the stock back up. I'll call you later," I said and hung up.

I arrived at the office at seven o'clock and spent the morning on the phone. Stockholders from across the country were demanding explanations for the stock's drop. At nine o'clock, I was served with the first of many stockholder class-action lawsuits. David Lundy called to tell me the SEC had begun investigating

ZZZZ Best. My twelve hundred employees desperately needed encouragement, but I was just too busy.

The investment firm investigators peppered me with questions about the credit card scam for most of the afternoon. Apparently Mike's and my stories didn't quite jibe. By three o'clock, the accounting firm had made the Dennis allegations known to everyone—including David Lundy. And at the closing bell, ZZZZ Best stock had dropped below ten dollars a share. I was overwhelmed by the pressure, but I refused to give in. ZZZZ Best was my sole reason for living. If it died, I died.

For the next twenty-four hours, I helped prepare a press release that I hoped would stop the stock's fall. I swore to Matt Paulson at the accounting firm that I had never had any financial dealings with Dennis and that none of his allegations had any validity. He was skeptical. Too many things were happening, and too many questions were still unanswered.

On Thursday, May 28, I got up at 3:55 A.M. to get to the office by 4:30. I had to call the wire service at least an hour before the market opened back east. It was dark and quiet as I pulled into ZZZZ Best headquarters. When I went to unlock the door, I realized I had forgotten my keys, but I didn't have time to go back to the house. There I was, standing alone in the ZZZZ Best parking lot at 4:30 in the morning with no keys and my whole company crumbling around me. "I should have gone to college!" I muttered as I smashed my elbow through a window.

In minutes I was on the phone, dictating a press release to the wire service. The press release implied that the investment banking firm's independent investigation had cleared the company of any wrongdoing. Though the stock had dipped below eight dollars a share, I was confident this announcement would turn the tide.

And when the market opened, the stock began to go up— slowly, but steadily. My confidence was suddenly restored. This seemed a sure sign of victory.

The L.A. law firm's investigators met with me again that morning. Instead of being intimidated, I answered their questions with confidence and enthusiasm. *They're not going to get rid of me without a fight!* I said to myself. When they left my office that morning to interview Carl Stowe and other ZZZZ Best employees, I was sure they believed me.

I spent the rest of the morning watching our stock creep back up to almost ten dollars a share, restoring the confidence of people like Byron Buckley and Lee Herring—at least temporarily.

❖ ❖ ❖

I spent most of that weekend on the phone with Thomas Meyer. The investment firm had threatened to pull out of the KeyServ financing because our press release implied that their investigators had cleared us. Meyer had fought hard to hold the deal together.

On Sunday evening, Miles Harris called me at home.

"Barry, our lawyers have advised us to terminate our agreement with you for the forty-million-dollar financing," he said sternly. "You'll have to make a public announcement early tomorrow morning."

"So all that time I spent with the investigators was for nothing?" I protested.

There was no arguing with him. I had to make the announcement and try to find another investment banker to do the financing.

❖ ❖ ❖

On Monday, June 1, I was once again at the office by 4:30 A.M. (this time with my keys). I knew that sending this new release over the wire would hurt my stock, but I had no choice. If I failed to disclose that the investment firm had terminated our agreement, I'd be in even deeper trouble with the SEC. The stock took a beating as the market opened, and dropped below seven dollars. While I worked on holding the company together, Meyer worked on getting another investment banker, without success.

Nonetheless, I couldn't give up. I had over twelve hundred employees depending on me and hundreds of stockholders hoping that there was enough Barry Minkow "magic" left to pull ZZZZ Best through yet another crisis. The lawyers who were still investigating insisted on examining all the company's canceled checks for the past two years. When confronted with the checks I made out to Robert Fuller, Phil Cox, and Stanley Robbins, I explained that these men had worked on the restoration projects, but the investigators weren't convinced. They also came up with two pages of questions and contradictions on the restoration files for Carl Stowe to resolve.

Another stumbling block I faced daily was the media. They smelled fraud, and just as a shark follows the scent of blood, they wouldn't stop digging until they had unearthed the truth. Some reporters even flew to Dallas, where I had recently claimed ZZZZ Best was doing $13.8 million in restoration work. There they contacted local newspapers, the city clerk's office, and even the Dallas Chamber of Commerce, trying to find a building that had recently suffered nearly $14 million in damage. When they found no corroborative evidence, they reported it. Once again I could do nothing—because there was no Dallas restoration job. The noose was tightening.

❖   ❖   ❖

"Did you write these checks?" asked Matt Paulson, placing two canceled checks on my desk. Many months earlier, Gary had asked me to lend a friend of his some money. I had written a couple of checks to Gary's friend and had promptly forgotten about it. Now it was coming back to haunt me. Paul Dennis was that friend!

I stared directly at my signature on the checks and said, "I don't remember offhand, Matt. I'll have to check."

Less than seventy-two hours later, Matt Paulson sent me a resignation letter. I had lost my accounting firm.

❖ ❖ ❖

During the next two weeks, the pressure mounted. Both Citizens Credit and Western Hills insistently demanded payment. News about the resignation of the accounting firm spread through the investment community and pushed the stock down even further. The lawyers who were investigating started to pose questions I couldn't answer. One concerned a letter sent by a "Mr. B. Cautious" to the accounting firm after they resigned. It contained a detailed explanation of the restoration fraud. *How in the world could anyone know so much?* I thought. If that wasn't bad enough, the money I had obtained from the New York investment firm and Pat Chapman was dwindling fast. But I was determined not to give up—not yet.

❖ ❖ ❖

Saturday morning, June 27, I was looking forward to spending the day with my girls' softball team at their tournament in San Fernando. We had qualified by taking our league championship. I thought back to the championship game as I sped down the freeway. It had been less than two months ago; it seemed like years. So much had happened in such a short time.

The phone rang. It was one of my board members.

"Barry, can you stop by my office? Several of us are here—and the attorneys, too; we need to talk to you."

"But I'm on my way to a big tournament."

"It'll only take ten minutes. Can you please come over?"

"All right. I'll be right there."

They're not calling me for an emergency meeting on a Saturday to give me a raise, I thought as I drove to the office. I arrived within fifteen minutes and greeted two of the investigating attorneys and several board members.

"Barry, we're sorry to call you in on such short notice, but we have a serious problem," one of the board members said. "The investigators have informed us that unless they are given the addresses to *all* the restoration jobs, they will not be able to complete their investigation." All eyes focused on me.

This is it, I thought. *I'm through.* I could do a lot of things, but I couldn't provide addresses for jobs that didn't exist. I had done my best to hold things together, but as soon as they made that demand, I knew it was over.

"No problem," I lied. "Give me until Wednesday or Thursday of next week, and you'll have every address of every job."

They all smiled, thinking that their problems were solved.

It took only a few minutes to get back on the freeway and head toward the softball tournament. My heart was beating rapidly as I planned how and when I would leave the company. *The press is going to jump all over this,* I thought. *I'll need a good criminal lawyer and as much cash as I can get my hands on.* I'd spend the first part of the week secretly withdrawing funds from the company. Then on Thursday or Friday, I would tender my resignation.

Several of the girls on my team ran up to greet me as I climbed out of my car. I was a hero to them. *Boy, are they going to be disappointed when they find out that ZZZZ Best was a fraud,* I thought. Then I thought about Byron Buckley, David Lundy, Vera Hojecki, Mike, my mom, and all the other employees who would shortly be out of work. I had failed them as well. And then I thought about prison.

❖ ❖ ❖

"I'll be happy to represent you," my attorney, John Pearson said. "You look awful, Barry. Why don't you go home and get some rest. I'll prepare the resignation letters and make sure they get to all the board members and Lundy by tomorrow morning."

It felt good to know I had at least one friend in the world—even though his "friendship" was costing me several hundred thousand dollars. But I was confident that he could defend me against any future prosecution. I left his office at 7:30 that warm, July 1 evening and headed for home.

Although I knew I was soon to become known as one of the most notorious con men in the United States, I felt a weird sense of relief. The fraud was about to be revealed. I no longer had to fear that call at two o'clock in the morning from some reporter saying, "We found out about the phony restoration business." It was ending, and for some strange reason, deep down in my heart, I was glad it was over.

On the Beach | 15

"Barry Minkow Steps Down as Chairman of ZZZZ Best" was front-page news on Friday, July 3, 1987, in *The New York Times, The Wall Street Journal,* and *USA Today.* Television news organizations from across the country besieged ZZZZ Best headquarters, trying to interview anyone who would talk about Barry Minkow, fraud, and his sudden demise. My dream of becoming famous had finally come true.

As I lay in my upstairs bedroom, watching these events unfold, I realized that my whole purpose for living had ceased to exist. I had no identity apart from ZZZZ Best. When I went out with friends or to parties, the topic of conversation had always been Barry Minkow and his "miracle" company. Now that I had failed, there was nothing to talk about. But it was worse than that. I wasn't just a failure—I had fallen, hurting thousands of people on the way down. Although I had tried for years to earn people's love, acceptance, and respect, now I'd be remembered as the kid who'd conned everyone . . . even my own mother, who now sat at home with no job. It was time to call her.

"Hi, Mom, it's Barry. Are you okay?"

"Well, I guess so," she said hesitantly. "The media is camped out on the front lawn, waiting for Dad and me to give an interview."

"Are you gonna talk to 'em?"

"Of course not, but you can't tell them that. How are you holding up under all this?"

I sighed. "Okay, I guess. But it's hard to watch everything I've worked for cave in so quickly."

"What does your attorney say? . . . Are you in a lot of trouble, son?"

"You know what, Mom, instead of talking about this over the phone, I'm going to come over. Is that okay?"

"Sure, Barry, if you don't mind dodging the press."

"I'll be there in fifteen minutes." I hung up the phone, turned off the TV, and ran down the stairs.

"Where are you going?" Donna asked.

"To Mom and Dad's. I'll be back in an hour and then we'll talk," I said, running out the door. I had waited until just two days ago to tell Donna that the person she'd lived with for the past three years, and thought she knew, was a fraud.

As soon as the gate opened, I saw the television cameras. They had surrounded the guard station, hoping to get an up-to-date clip of the now-infamous con man. Even though I knew I'd be cast in a negative light, deep inside I wanted to stop and let them shoot. Being on television was like a drug to me. My first time on camera had been like a junkie's first injection—the minute it hit my "vein," I was addicted. I resisted the temptation and headed toward my parents' house. It felt weird, driving in midmorning with no long appointment schedule or the car phone ringing off the hook.

I made it past the media and was sitting alone with Mom in her bedroom fifteen minutes later. She had a worried look on her face.

"You look like you haven't slept in two months," she said.

"I haven't."

She laughed then and took control of the conversation. "I know why you're here, Barry. You feel sorry for me and want to apologize for my present unemployment." She paused, waiting for me to stop looking out the window at the press. "I have a confession to make to you—if you want to hear it."

"Of course I do, Mom." I sat on the floor next to the bed. "But what could *you* possibly have to confess to *me?*"

"Well, do you remember about a year or so ago when I asked you about going to heaven?"

"Yeah," I lied. I made it a point not to remember "religious" conversations.

"You said, 'How much is God? I'll buy him.'"

That jarred my memory. "Oh yeah, I remember that, Mom. I hope you weren't offended by that comment."

"After that conversation I did something you're not going to like. . . . I began to pray for the demise of ZZZZ Best."

"You did what, Mom?" Was she crazy? Who would pray for the failure of the company that fed her family?

"Don't get me wrong, Barry. I didn't do it to hurt you or get you in trouble. I did it because I love you and because I realized you would never consider changing unless you and ZZZZ Best parted company." She looked at me intently, waiting for a response.

I went to the window and stared out at the reporters. *My own mother was against me,* I thought to myself. *And she had even enlisted God!* I felt betrayed.

"Listen, I want you to know I'm not going to give you some long lecture on what you should or shouldn't have done with ZZZZ Best. That's over and done with," she said earnestly. "But I do want to tell you that my offer about heaven still stands. God loves you, Barry. He knows what your deepest needs are, and He's willing and waiting to forgive you."

I ran my fingers through my hair and began to pace nervously. Could God really love me? Could He satisfy my deepest needs, even though I had hurt so many people?

"So what do you want me to do, Mom?" I asked.

"I want you to talk with someone about your situation. Because I'm your mother, you probably wouldn't feel comfortable talking to me. So I have someone else in mind."

It was an interesting idea. I did need someone I could talk to, someone who would listen. "Who?"

"Maggie."

I should have known. Maggie Clay had been my Mom's Christian counselor for many years. Mom saw her every week, and many in the family respected the change Maggie had helped to bring about in Mom's life. Maggie must be near retirement age; I had known her since I was seven, and I had always liked her.

"All right, Mom, I'll go see her. Will you set up an appointment for me?"

Her answer was surprising. "No, I won't. I want you to do that yourself."

I glanced at my watch and remembered that my attorney wanted me to call him. I walked toward the door. "Okay, Mom. I'll call and set up an appointment on my way home." I couldn't leave without thanking her. "Thanks for not kicking me when I'm down. . . . I love you."

❖ ❖ ❖

"ZZZZ Best Files for Bankruptcy" was the radio announcer's lead story as I drove to see Maggie. I was glad the July Fourth weekend had ended. Usually I enjoyed the summer holiday, but not this time. Too many things had gone wrong. Almost immediately after my resignation, the stock had fallen to zero, and the SEC had halted trading in ZZZZ Best. I knew it wouldn't be long before the company went under. Before I resigned, I took out almost $700,000. I gave my attorney a generous retainer, hired a private investigator to work on my defense, and earmarked the balance for discreet business investments that I hoped would provide me with enough money to live on.

When I arrived at Maggie's, she greeted me warmly and led me into a small, nicely decorated room. I sat in a comfortable reclining chair, occasionally sipping from a can of cola and staring at the picture of Jesus on the wall next to her chair from time to time. I felt safe in her small place, temporarily removed from the media and the many people I had victimized.

After about an hour of getting reacquainted and talking about old times, Maggie asked, "What are you really here for, Barry?"

"I don't know, Maggie. I guess I want what you and my mom have got," I replied casually.

"And what might that be?" she pressed.

I thought for a moment. "Peace, happiness, contentment—to be able to look at myself in the mirror without feeling guilty." Maggie listened attentively. "On the other hand, I don't want to go to jail. Or . . ." Suddenly, unaccountably, I wanted to be honest with her—and with myself. "Maybe I'm here because becoming a Christian might earn me some sympathy with the media or some future jury."

She was smiling. "Well, Barry, after listening to you for the last hour, I've made a few preliminary observations. Want to hear them?"

"Of course."

"No one's going to convince me that when you were sixteen years old and started ZZZZ Best, you *planned* on using it to rip off Wall Street. I knew you back then, and I just can't believe that was your original intention. But as the company grew, so did your ego. Your mother told me all about your escapades, and I watched you on television. You got caught in the vain pursuit of money, power, and fame."

Had she ever hit the nail on the head! Had I known that ZZZZ Best would end like this, I would never have accepted Jerry's offer back on that evening in 1982.

"The best thing you've got going for you right now is your

desire to be honest with me. By telling me the truth about why you're here, you've confirmed to me that you have potential."

"Yeah, but what do I do now?" I asked. "I have trouble sleeping at night because I feel so guilty about what I did. Every time I turn on the TV, some reporter is guessing how many years I'll spend in prison, and wherever I go, people stare at me and snarl. It's tough, Maggie." I fought back tears.

"I'm not going to preach to you, Barry, but I do want to give you three simple things to remember. They're not profound— just simple truths that will help you. Are you ready to hear them?"

"Yeah," I said, my voice cracking.

"Good. The first thing I want you to know is that it's never too late to start doing what's right. Sound easy enough? Even though you've spent most of the first twenty-one years of your life doing what's wrong, the message of Christianity—and Jesus in particular—is that it's never too late to start doing what's right.

"Secondly, forgiveness will overcome your feelings of guilt." She waited until I looked at her before she continued. "Guilt is real, and people will use all kinds of drugs and gimmicks to escape it, but in reality the knowledge of divine forgiveness is the only solution to the problem of guilt.

"Finally, if you accept God's forgiveness by receiving His Son, you need to realize that although the Lord will not deliver you *from* the consequences of your actions, he will give you the strength and protection to make it *through* them."

"What do you mean by that?" I asked quietly.

"I mean that you may have to go to jail, but if you do, He will be right next to you through the whole ordeal. In fact, the Bible tells us that Jesus is 'a friend who sticks closer than a brother.'"

"I always wanted a brother, Maggie."

She chuckled. "I'm not going to pressure you into making

any hasty decisions, Barry, but I would like you to consider seeing me at least twice a week, if that's okay with you."

"That's fine with me. . . . I'd like that."

❖   ❖   ❖

"Let's walk down the street," said Phil Cox. "I think your house is bugged." This was my first contact with my former associates since my resignation. I was scared, but I knew I'd have to face them sooner or later.

I thought back to Maggie's words: "Although the Lord will not deliver you from the consequences of your actions, He'll give you the strength and protection to make it through them." *If You're up there, God, I could use some of that protection now,* I said to myself as Phil and I walked the streets of Westchester County Estates.

"Well, Phil, tell me, do I need to look over my shoulder for the rest of my life?" I asked respectfully.

"No, kid, not if you do the right thing."

"And what might 'the right thing' be?"

"We want you to blame everything on Ron Knox. That's your defense . . . blame it on Knox." Knox had recently died undergoing open-heart surgery, making him the perfect scapegoat.

"Anything else I should know?"

"Yeah, as long as you don't go to any grand juries, you're all right. Defend yourself *against* the Feds any way you want. But don't work *with* them, or you'll have problems. . . . No one likes a rat."

"Will I see you again?"

"No, I'm going back east. There's too much heat around here. Just do as I told you and you'll be okay, kid. . . . Good luck to you."

That's it? Just "do the right thing" and "see ya later"? No offer to help with my legal expenses? That's what I wanted to say, but I kept quiet and watched Phil Cox drive out of my driveway, and out of my life. My relationship with this group of people ended as it had begun—in the blink of an eye.

❖   ❖   ❖

"Thanks for encouraging me to see Maggie, Mom. We really had a wonderful time. She's a great lady!" I said from my BMW car phone as I drove toward the beach. After meeting with Phil, I wanted to go somewhere where I could be alone and sort some things out in my mind. Several months before, Donna and I had discovered a secluded cove in Malibu, across from a favorite restaurant.

"She sure is, Barry. She's been around for a long time and has a way of getting right to the point," Mom added.

"I'm going to see her on a regular basis."

"Good for you. I'm proud of you, Barry."

"Thanks. Is Dad okay?"

"He'll be fine. The question is, are *you?*"

"I think so, Mom. For some strange reason, I think I *will* be."

Thirty minutes later, I was at the beach. The sun had set and, because it was a weeknight, few people were about. I made my way over the rocks and sat on the dry sand. The bright moonlight shimmered off the water as the waves crashed against the shore. I looked up and saw the stars against a dark sky. I had contemplated fleeing the country to solve my problems, but after seeing Maggie, that was no longer an option. "It's never too late to start doing what's right," she had said.

I walked to the edge of the shore and picked up a few rocks and tossed them out into the water. I recalled the days in the garage with Mom, Vera, and Mike. I missed them and wondered if Vera and Mike would ever forgive me. I knew Mom already had.

My mind raced back to my twenty-first birthday party with all those people crowded into my house, paying their respects to the guy with the fat checkbook. Now the money was gone, and so were the crowds. Then there were all those letters from fans across the country, in the nightstand next to my bed. They had all declared, "I want to be just like you, Barry Minkow!" Well, I had let them all down.

The water washed over my feet as I began to walk along the shore. I remembered the tone of Ron's voice when he had confronted me about the money orders. I had let him down too. I thought about Doug Fitzgerald, and the time and effort he had invested in trying to make me into a legitimate businessman. But I had chosen a different route.

I stopped walking, sat down, and began to cry. What if Stan decided I couldn't be trusted to fight the government? What would he do? I remembered the convention and ZZZZ Best managers chanting, "Barry . . . Barry . . . Barry . . ." Now they were unemployed, and it was my fault. The tears dripped off my face onto the sand. I thought about prison and how dangerous it was there. Prison scenes in movies depicted violence and horrible living conditions. That's where I was headed. I remembered the simple question Maggie had asked me as I left her house: "Did it *work,* Barry? Did all the women, money, and fame bring you true happiness and contentment?" She knew they hadn't. When the cameras weren't rolling and the lights were off and everyone had gone home, I was always alone with my guilt, shame, and loneliness. It was time to cut my losses and make a change.

In desperation, I began to pray. "Dear God, or Jesus, or whoever You are," I muttered as I looked up into the clear, starry sky, "I've made a mess of my life, but I suppose You already know that. I need Your help. If You're anything like Maggie and

Mom say You are, then I ask that You forgive me and help me change. I've been a liar for so many years I'm not sure that this isn't just another one of my cons. I'm afraid of prison and maybe that's my true motive. But if You do exist, please make this prayer real in my life by changing me."

When I finished, no lightning came down from above. There were no spectacular signs. The waves continued to break and the traffic continued to race along Pacific Coast Highway. But that evening, a lonely, distraught, twenty-one-year-old boy began a relationship with Jesus Christ.

❖ ❖ ❖

"You're not going to jail," my attorney proclaimed in his tastefully decorated office. "It's not like you killed anybody. There's no jury in the world that will convict a twenty-one-year-old kid of pulling off a sophisticated white-collar crime. They'll realize that you were used."

"But what about the media? They seem to think that I'm going to prison—and for a long time," I protested. I wanted to believe John, wanted to believe that I could walk away from the ZZZZ Best fraud unscathed! I even sold my Ferrari to increase my defense fund. Nevertheless, I still had doubts, because I knew I was guilty.

"That's because they haven't heard your side of the story yet, Barry." John got up from his desk and walked to a small table holding a coffee machine. He poured himself a freshly brewed cup and returned to his chair. "I got a call from *60 Minutes* this morning. They want to do an interview with you." He waited for my reaction; there was none. "They want to send Diane Sawyer out in a few weeks to speak with me, and with you, of course."

I was skeptical. "Do you really think we should do an interview for them? Those guys from *60 Minutes* are brutal. They could make me look really bad!"

"Or they could make you look innocent," he quickly added. "If you can look that camera right in the eye and put enough of that Barry Minkow charm into it, you'll be able to persuade all America that you're innocent."

The idea appealed to me. I didn't want the American people to view me as the greatest con man of the twentieth century. But then, I didn't want to go to prison, either. It was worth the gamble.

"Okay, let's do it. I've got one more con left in me."

❖   ❖   ❖

"Thank you, Maggie. I love it!" I said, inspecting the new Bible she had just handed me. "Where should I start reading?"

"That's up to you, Barry. But I'd start with the gospel of John in the New Testament."

After some small talk, we sat down and began the session. First, I told Maggie about my trip to the beach. I explained how I had asked for God's forgiveness and His help to change. She was overjoyed to hear of my conversion. But when I told her about my meeting with my attorney and the *60 Minutes* interview, she had a change of attitude.

"Now, Barry, you just got through telling me that you wanted God to change you, and yet here you are taking matters into your own hands again."

"What do you mean?" I asked.

"You're going to go on national television and lie! You can't do that and expect people to believe that you've changed."

Her words cut through my rationalizations. "Well, what do you want me to do, Maggie? If I take your advice, I'm definitely going to jail, right?"

"Maybe—maybe not. I can't give you any guarantees. But if I were in your position, I'd simply tell the truth and let the chips fall where they may," she advised. "Don't resort to lying and manipulating like you have for so many years. Just do what's right and let God work out the details."

"That's easier said than done."

"Perhaps, but that's why I gave you that book. You'll find all the direction you need in there." She was pointing to my new Bible.

❖   ❖   ❖

"Over to your left you'll see the actual house where *Psycho* was filmed," said the voice on the intercom. A friend thought I needed to get my mind off ZZZZ Best and the media, which continued to cover my fall. What better way to do that than a trip to Universal Studios? Perhaps the greatest disadvantage of running a business between the ages of sixteen and twenty-one was the lack of time I'd had for things like amusement parks.

As the studio tram progressed along its route, I attempted to sort out all that was happening. It was now early September—two months since my resignation—but I still hadn't been indicted.

My attorney had told me that Carl Stowe and Jerry Williams were cooperating with the U.S. Attorney's office, telling all and hoping for leniency. "You can expect to be arrested any day now," he warned.

I couldn't blame Carl and Jerry for turning on me. My abrupt resignation had made their lives miserable.

The *60 Minutes* interview was only a few weeks away. Despite Maggie's advice, I had decided to go through with it. *This will be my last con,* I swore to myself. As soon as the interview helped me avoid prison, my career as a con man would come to an end.

Money was quickly becoming a problem. After some bad business investments and payments to my attorney, the funds I had taken from the company were rapidly dwindling. Since I couldn't get a job—who's going to hire a con man who has buried a three-hundred-million-dollar public company?—I needed to think of a way to earn a living. Then I remembered the steam cleaner and chemicals I had stored in my garage. If I could persuade Mom to do the telephone soliciting, I could easily go out and do the work. But what if I were recognized? Since the ZZZZ Best collapse, my picture had been plastered all over the media. I needed a disguise.

By the time the tour ended, I had devised a plan that I hoped would keep me out of jail, put food on the table, and perhaps even take my mind off a prospectively frightening future.

❖   ❖   ❖

Boy, is this book boring, I said to myself as I slogged through the one chapter a day I had promised Maggie. Though I enjoyed and looked forward to our twice-weekly meetings, reading the Bible without her there to explain it was difficult.

I glanced at the clock next to my bed and realized I was late for the first carpet-cleaning appointment of the day. I rushed into the bathroom, washed my face, and reached into the top drawer for my hidden stash of steroids. Maggie's words pricked my conscience: "You're not still taking steroids, are you, Barry?" My answer was always the same: "Of course not, Maggie." In reality, since my resignation I had increased my daily dosage. Fearing what could happen to me if I had to go to prison, I worked out harder and took more steroids to prepare myself.

After getting dressed, I put on my carpet-cleaning disguise— an old pair of large-framed reading glasses and a baseball cap that came down over my ears. I set out for the first appointment of the day with my partner, a longtime family friend who was still there for me even when the money and fame were gone. Mom usually lined up two or three jobs a day for us, and this particular October day was no different.

"What's going to happen to the house?" he asked as we drove to the first job.

"Well, I'll probably lose it, along with everything else," I said. "I can no longer afford to pay a five-thousand-dollar-a-month mortgage."

"Somehow it doesn't seem fair, Barry." For years you worked night and day, trying to build ZZZZ Best, only to see it fall apart in a matter of weeks."

I smiled and put my hand on his shoulder. "There's a little more to it than that. One of these days I'll sit down and tell you all about it."

We pulled into the driveway of a large home, where a pleasant woman greeted us at the door and showed us the areas she wanted cleaned. We unloaded the equipment and proceeded to clean her lightly soiled beige carpeting.

"So, what do you think of this ZZZZ Best ordeal?" the lady asked me as I poured a five-gallon bucket of clean water into the machine. "Since you're in the business, you must have heard about this Barry Minkow kid."

I pulled down my baseball cap and turned my head. *Man, I hope she doesn't recognize me,* I said to myself, nearly panicking. "I've heard of the guy," I replied with my back to her, pretending to wipe off the machine.

"I think it's a tragedy. All those stockholders lost their money! I hope that kid goes to jail for a long time! What do you think?" she pressed.

Her words caught me off guard. Here was a woman I didn't even know who wanted to see me go to prison. I felt like asking her how she would have handled people like Knox, Snyder, Robbins, and Cox. "Well, I'm kind of interested in hearing *his* side of the story," I said. It felt strange talking about myself to someone who didn't know who I was.

"I don't know," the woman went on. "There seems to be a lot of evidence against him . . . what with all those phony contracts. . . . That kid's probably got millions of dollars stashed away!"

"You'll have to excuse me, ma'am. I left some chemicals in the truck." I walked to the truck and hurled a gallon bottle of shampoo against the tailgate. *Rats!* I said to myself. *This stupid woman thinks I've got millions buried somewhere! I wish I could sit her down and explain how I tried to use the millions of dollars I raised to keep the company running until January of 1988.* It wasn't until five days before I resigned that I took money I never intended to pay back. And now even that was gone!

As I leaned against the truck, it dawned on me that this lady probably represented the prevailing public opinion. People honestly believed that I had stashed away enough money to last me the rest of my life. And here I was cleaning carpets, struggling to survive.

Not wanting to raise suspicion, I went back in the house and switched places with my partner. Normally he pushed the wand and I filled the machine, but to avoid further conversation, I gladly pushed the wand and thought about her remarks.

❖ ❖ ❖

"So, what you're saying, Mr. Minkow, is that while all this fraud was going on with the restoration business, you were busy with the carpet-cleaning stores and the stockholders?" Diane Sawyer asked, as we sat in my living room.

My attorney was behind the camera, monitoring my every comment. Donna sat out of the way on the staircase, watching the action. I glanced over at her before I answered Sawyer's question.

"That's right, ma'am," I lied.

"So you didn't know the Sacramento job was a fraud?" Sawyer asked.

I thought about Maggie and our meetings. For the past five months, she had prayed that I would stop lying. *It's never too late to start doing what's right* burned in my mind. Then I thought of the horrors of prison—the killings, rape, drugs, and violence—that awaited me if I didn't lie. *Donna won't wait for me if I get sent to prison,* I thought. *I'm sure I'll lose her!*

"No, I didn't know the Sacramento job was phony—or any other job for that matter," I replied.

Diane Sawyer looked astonished. She knew the truth. She had done interviews and reviewed the evidence. "What about your alleged involvement with the underworld? Is there any truth to those claims?" she probed.

"No, ma'am," I replied quickly, squirming in my chair.

I recalled my trip to the beach, back in July, when my tears had dripped onto the sand and I had begged God to change me. It had taken me only until November to forsake that commitment.

Sawyer looked at me intently, pulled a document from a file folder, and placed it in front of me. "Then, can you explain why you and an alleged associate of an underworld family were partners in a business venture?"

"That's not correct, ma'am. We weren't partners in any company," I said, recalling my last meeting with Philip Cox.

"Is that so? Then can you explain why your signature is on the articles of incorporation of that company—and why this man signed as president of that company?"

I looked at my attorney, but couldn't catch his eye. The cameras were rolling and the bright lights were making me sweat. The evidence was overwhelming—I was guilty. Maggie was right: I should have told the truth. But for Barry Minkow, that was a difficult thing to do, especially with the cameras rolling.

"That's not my signature, ma'am," I countered. "It's a forgery."

❖ ❖ ❖

"Hello?" I said in a groggy voice.

"Barry, this is Roland Smith. Are you okay?" The last person

I thought I'd receive a call from in my hospital bed was a government agent involved in the ZZZZ Best investigation.

"Yeah, Roland, I'm all right," I replied softly.

"They tell me you almost died the other night. Is that true?"

"I don't know. . . . I guess I had a bad case of pneumonia. The fever got out of hand and, because I was vomiting so much, I got dangerously dehydrated. I'll be okay, though."

"Well, that's good to hear. Will you be out of the hospital before Christmas?"

"Why do you ask?"

I had run into Roland Smith a few times between July and December of 1987. He had questioned me, but he was always courteous and respectful. He stayed objective throughout the ZZZZ Best investigation and treated it like any other. I really believe he called me because he cared.

Roland went on . . . "You're not still taking those steroids, are you?" Interviewing everybody I had ever known had made Roland Smith an expert on my past and present activities. He knew I took massive doses of anabolic steroids, and he also knew they were the cause of many of my health problems.

"Of course not, Roland," I lied.

"Well, I'm going to let you get some rest. I hope you feel better, Barry . . . and I mean that."

When I hung up the phone I stared at the IV running into my forearm. *I'm killing myself with these steroids,* I said to myself, *just as I did during the* 60 Minutes *interview* (which was due to air in early January).

As I lay in that hospital bed, I remembered what Maggie had said to me during our last counseling session: "You are your own worst enemy, Barry."

I fought to sit up, but I was too weak. *Lord, please help me— I'm killing myself and I can't change. Please take over my life . . . before I lose it.*

PART 4:
Comeback

If the Shoe Fits | 16

Put your hands behind your back and stand against the wall," barked the police officer.

"Hey, wait a minute," protested my attorney. "The kid turned himself in. You don't need to treat him like that."

"Look, Pearson, he's in our custody now. We'll treat him like we do any other criminal!"

The deal was simple: The government would call my attorney when the indictment was handed down, and he would drive me to a downtown police station called "The Glass House," where I would be booked and hopefully released on bail. It was Thursday evening, January 14, 1988, when John received the phone call.

As the officer cuffed my hands behind my back and led me down a long hallway, I heard John say, "Don't worry, Barry, I'll have you out by tomorrow morning." I hoped he was right.

"Step in here," the officer ordered. He closed the door behind us and unlocked my handcuffs. "Take your clothes off."

"What?" I said, thinking I had misunderstood him.

"You heard me—take 'em off . . . now!"

I reached for my shoelaces. I thought about my Mom and Maggie. When they'd found out that I had been indicted, they had promised to pray for me. The shoes came off. I remembered the lady at the *Northridger* who had asked me, back in 1982, if I was in business for myself or if I had a partner. "I'm the sole owner of the company," I had replied. The socks came off. I recalled my first meeting with Ron Knox at his town house. Now he was dead, and I wished I were too! My shirt came off. As I started to unfasten my pants, I looked up and saw the officer staring at me intently. He seemed to be amused by the show. "If you get in my way, I'll run you over!" was what I had said less than three years before to the manager of the competing carpet-cleaning company who had tried to steal my technicians. I pulled off my pants and boxer shorts and threw them in front of me. The officer watched me carefully. "Wonder Boy Falls from Grace"—one of the many recent headlines—came to mind. As I stood there naked in that cold, musty room, I realized nothing was worth this kind of humiliation. Not even ZZZZ Best.

"Put your hands over your head!" he yelled. I complied.

"Run your fingers through your hair and open your mouth," he ordered. "So, you're the great Barry Minkow I keep reading about! When you had all that money, did you ever think that one day you'd be standing naked in a police station?" He laughed. This mockery was one of the "consequences" Maggie had warned me about. "Now turn around and let me see the bottoms of your feet."

"Come on, man, I ain't got nothin' under my *feet*," I protested.

"Look, pal, you'll do as you're told, or I'll get five officers in here to make you!" Once again I complied.

"Put your clothes back on," he ordered.

I hadn't been in jail more than fifteen minutes, and I already hated it.

❖   ❖   ❖

"I'm setting bail at $2.2 million," said the magistrate from her bench in the downtown Los Angeles courthouse.

"But, your honor, Mr. Minkow is broke and could never

come up with that kind of money. Besides, he's no flight risk. He turned himself in, knowing for over six months that he was going to be indicted," my attorney protested.

"I'm aware of that, Mr. Pearson, but considering the magnitude of the offense, I think $2.2 million is more than fair. . . . This court is adjourned!"

The marshals handcuffed me and rushed me out of the courtroom. As we marched to a holding tank, reporters ran to keep up, yelling out, "Are they treating you all right?" "Are you going to plead guilty?"

Carl Stowe, Gary Todd, and Jerry Williams were also indicted, but they were released on bail. Robert Fuller, Phil Cox, Stanley Robbins, and Alan Hoffman were *not* arrested or charged in the ZZZZ Best case. *At least I don't have to worry about them,* I thought as I paced the small cell. My plans for making bail and spending the weekend in the free world were shattered. *I hope You haven't forgotten about me, Lord,* I prayed.

"Hey, Minkow, we're taking you to Terminal Island," one of the marshals told me.

"Where's that?"

"It's in Long Beach . . . ocean-front property!" he joked.

The indictment charged me with fifty-four counts of stock fraud, mail fraud, tax evasion, and bank fraud. Since each count potentially carried a five-year sentence, I faced 270 years in prison. It was time for me to start praying again.

❖ ❖ ❖

I tossed and turned through my first night at Terminal Island on a small bunk bed in the middle of a long corridor. Like most federal prisons, Terminal Island was overcrowded. They were out of pillows, and the one blanket they had issued me failed to protect me from the cold sea air.

Although I tried to maintain a low profile, word had spread

rapidly through the prison that Barry Minkow, "The ZZZZ Best Man," had arrived. My first day a man came up to me in the yard and said, "Hey, I should kick your teeth in, punk! My mother lost big money in your stock!" Other guys watched to see how I would react. I glanced at the gun towers overlooking the yard and wondered if I'd get caught if I hit him. But I remembered my prayer from my hospital bed: *Lord, please change me.* Fighting and arguing were *old* ways of handling problems, and, as Maggie had said, "It's never too late to start doing what's right."

"Hey, man, I'm really sorry about that. It was never my intention to hurt anyone—especially your mother," I said sincerely, never losing eye contact.

My response caught him off guard. He turned and walked away.

It didn't take long for me to return to my old ways, though. After my first week in prison, I went on a search for anabolic steroids. I knew from past experience that if I didn't keep taking the drug, I'd lose both muscle mass and strength. That scared me, especially being surrounded by over thirteen hundred men.

While I waited for someone to sneak the steroids in through the visiting room, I started learning karate. Two Black Muslims offered to teach and train me for forty dollars a month. Since they were both black belts, and because I felt the need to protect myself, I agreed.

My attorney visited me at least twice a week, always holding out hope that I would get a bail reduction and be out soon. He also told me that I had been assigned a federal judge. "His name is Dickran Tevrizian, Barry, and he's supposed to be fair."

"Will he let me out on a reasonable bail?"

"That's what we're going to find out. We have a hearing set in early February. Meanwhile, stay out of trouble and try to adjust."

❖ ❖ ❖

"Hi, Mom, it's me," I said, making one of my daily calls to her. "I got your letter and appreciate your prayers." She didn't respond. "What's wrong, Mom?"

There was another long pause before she spoke. "I don't quite know how to tell you this, Barry. . . ."

"Tell me what?"

"It's about Maggie. . . . She's had a major stroke. She's in critical condition."

My stomach got queasy and I felt light-headed. Maggie Clay, the woman who had meant so much to me during the toughest time of my life, might be dying. I had to know. "Is she going to live, Mom?" I asked, fighting back tears.

"They say yes, but her whole right side is paralyzed, and she'll probably never talk again."

I tried to speak, but I couldn't. And I couldn't cry; there were too many people around. I had to hang up and find a place to be alone. "Mom, I've got to go now. I'll call you later."

I hung up the phone and ran to the movie auditorium. It was empty, except for a man sweeping the floor. I pulled a chair over to a dark corner and began to cry. I thought back to our many counseling sessions and all the times Maggie had said, "I love you," when the rest of the world despised me. I remembered the look on her face when I told her about my experience at the beach. As I cried, I realized I was doing the one thing Maggie had tried to teach me—to care for someone other than Barry Minkow.

❖ ❖ ❖

"Barry Minkow, report to the lieutenant's office. Barry Minkow to the lieutenant's office," proclaimed the voice over the loudspeaker. As I walked from the weight-lifting area, I wondered why the lieutenant wanted to see me. The steroids? No, the guy hadn't even given them to me yet. Maybe I had forgotten to make my bed. It wasn't unusual to be hauled in for neglecting a daily chore.

"Mr. Minkow, please empty out your pockets for me," ordered the lieutenant. "Just set the contents on my desk."

"I don't have anything in my pockets." The lieutenant was about five foot eight, but weighed over 250 pounds, I wasn't about to try to con him. "May I ask what this is all about?"

"Yes," he said, sitting down. "I'm going to put you in the 'hole' until I can complete an investigation."

"Investigation? What have I done?"

"We found a guard's uniform in an air duct near your bunk. Until we find out who put it there, we need to isolate you."

"I don't believe this! *I* didn't put it there."

"Apparently someone was going to use it to try to make an escape."

"Well, that's ridiculous, lieutenant," I argued. "I turned myself in. Why would I try to escape?"

"I don't know, Mr. Minkow, but until I find out, you're going to the hole."

❖   ❖   ❖

"Officer, could you come here please?" I called.

I didn't mind "doing time" at Terminal Island. The outdoor yard was big, and I was able to work out and practice karate. But the hole was different. After just one night locked up in that five-by-seven-foot cell with a bunk bed, toilet, and sink, I wanted out—back on the yard.

"Listen, can you please tell the lieutenant I want to see him. It's important," I said, poking my head through the small opening in the steel door.

"All right, I'll tell him," the officer replied.

In twenty minutes I was being escorted, with my hands cuffed behind my back, to the office.

"Look, Lieutenant," I began, "I want to try that uniform on to prove to you that I couldn't have stolen it. I've got to get out of that hole—there's no sunlight in there!"

"That's why we call it the 'hole,' Mr. Minkow. Now, are you sure you want to try it on? You don't have to. You might further incriminate yourself," he warned.

"I'm aware of that. Now, can I try it on?"

He motioned for the guard to unlock my handcuffs. I knew the uniform couldn't possibly fit me. Because of my muscular build, I had to have clothes custom-made. I quickly pulled off the bright orange jumpsuit (standard attire for the hole) and put on the gray button-down shirt.

"Looks like it fits pretty good, Minkow," he commented.

"An extra large shirt will fit most people in this place. The pants are what count."

I grabbed the khaki-style pants and pulled them on. My heart stopped. The length and waist fit perfectly! I looked at the lieutenant as he examined the tailor-made fit. When his eyes met mine, I pulled down the pants as fast as I could and said, "I want to see my attorney."

That night, they released all the inmates who had been put in the hole for the investigation. All, that is, except me.

❖ ❖ ❖

"Minkow, you've got a legal visit!" a guard screamed one morning as he pounded on the steel door.

I got up slowly, having spent much of the night thinking about my many problems, one of which I believed was my lawyer. I had decided finally that I needed to hire a new one. Several inmates told me I needed a lawyer with experience and knowledge of federal law. Though John had handled several state cases, his federal experience was limited.

The guard cuffed my hands behind my back and escorted me to the end of a dark corridor, where he unlocked a door and let me into the legal visiting area.

"Why are you dressed in that ugly jumpsuit, Barry?" John asked.

"Because I'm in the hole," I said, as I sat down across the desk from him. "They think I was planning to escape."

"That's ridiculous!" he argued. "You turned yourself in."

"I know, but they found a guard's uniform in a ceiling vent near my bunk. And since it fit me, they think I hid it there."

"How do they know it—?"

"Don't ask!" I interrupted him. "It's a long story." I got up from the chair and began to pace. "Look, John, I've been thinking things over, and I've decided I want to hire a new lawyer."

"Don't be absurd, Barry. I'm your lawyer!"

"It's not that I don't appreciate you, but I need someone with federal experience. I'm facing 270 years—not to mention a possible attempted escape charge—and I want someone who knows how to deal with these Feds."

"You're not thinking straight. I've got all the experience you'll ever need."

"I'm not going to argue with you, John. I've made up my mind."

"Who are you planning to hire?"

"I don't know yet."

After a brief discussion of financial matters—whether or not any of the retainer funds were still available—John picked up his leather briefcase and left the room, back to the free world.

The guards escorted me back to my cell and, once there, I lay on my bunk and started to cry. My world was caving in all around me. Everyone hated me, the government was trying to bury me, Maggie was paralyzed for life, I was about to be charged with attempted escape, and I had no lawyer to defend me against a fifty-four-count indictment. With all other options gone, I reached across the bunk and picked up the Bible Maggie had given me. Luckily, books were allowed in the hole. I was still crying when it fell open to Psalm 56. I read it slowly:

> *Be merciful to me, O God, for men hotly pursue me;*
> *all day long they press their attack.*
> *My slanderers pursue me all day long;*
> *many are attacking me in their pride.*
> *When I am afraid,*
> *I will trust in you.*

I kept reading down to verse 8, where it said:

> *Record my lament;*
> *list my tears on your scroll—*
> *are they not in your record?*

I wiped my tears on that very page of the Bible, hoping, perhaps, that it would bring me comfort. I prayed again: "Lord, please help me. Everything is collapsing all around me and I need Your help and comfort."

My prayer was interrupted by a man calling from the next cell. "Hey, Barry . . . Barry . . . can you hear me?"

I got up from my bunk and went to the air vent above the toilet.

"Hey, man. . . . I'm your next-door neighbor. I heard what they're trying to do to you. Are you all right?"

"I've been better," I spoke through the vent, my voice breaking.

"I read about your case in the papers. I've got a lot of respect for you. You're a real stand-up guy," he said. "Listen, I run this section of the hole. Do you need the phone or anything?"

"Yeah, if you can get it for me. I didn't know we could use the phone in here."

"Just leave it to me."

We talked throughout the afternoon. Hearing this man's story made my problems seem small. The government was accusing him of being the leader-organizer of a major drug ring—and of murder.

Later, a guard passed the phone to me through the trapdoor. After making a few calls, I felt better. Before I went to sleep that night, I read a few more passages in the Bible. This time the Book didn't seem boring at all.

❖ ❖ ❖

Bang! Bang! Bang! A loud noise woke me from a deep sleep. I got up quickly and looked through the food trap to see if I could make out where the noise was coming from. A man named Lopez, in a cell labeled "Three-man Hold"—at least three guards had to be present whenever his cell door was opened— was pounding on his steel door, moving it noticeably with his fists. The guard had given him a regular breakfast instead of his special meal (he had a delicate medical condition), and he had thrown the food down the hall and was screaming at the guard. Mr. Lopez was a very violent man.

Man, I'm just a white-collar criminal, and they've got me locked up with all these killers and crazy people, I said to myself. *What if this guy breaks down the door? He'll come right across the hall and get me next.*

Suddenly there was silence, and then I heard Lopez say to the guard, "You jerk! And you don't even have a mustache!"

Mustache? I thought. *Must be some kind of requirement for acceptance around this place.*

A guard delivered the correct breakfast to Lopez, which immediately silenced him.

Then I ran my finger across my upper lip and thought, *I*

don't have a mustache either! Later that day, when a guard asked me if I wanted to take a shower—it had been three days since my last one—I considered my clean-shaven upper lip again and decided to chance it.

As the guard led me to the shower in my boxer shorts with my hands cuffed behind my back, I sucked in my stomach and flexed as many muscles as I could. Lopez was watching me through his trapdoor. In the toughest voice I could muster, I said, "What's up, Lopez?"

"Not much," he replied.

"My lawyer made me shave my mustache. He wants me to look young for the trial. I feel naked without it," I said pointedly.

Lopez nodded his agreement. "I know what you mean, man. These Feds sure know how to hassle a guy!"

"Take it easy," I said to Lopez as we moved out of earshot.

❖　❖　❖

A loud knock on my cell door startled me. "Can't you guys knock quietly?" I protested.

"I'll do better next time," the guard joked. "Now get ready . . . ya got a legal visit."

Since I had parted ways with my attorney, I wondered who would be visiting me. Two sharply dressed men were waiting for me when I arrived in the legal visiting area. After a brief introduction I learned they were lawyers.

Apparently someone had referred them to me. We sat down and I explained to them my legal needs and the situation with the officer's uniform. They listened intently as I talked, and asked questions only for clarification.

At the conclusion of our nearly four-hour meeting, I confessed, "I know the whole world thinks I've got millions buried somewhere, but the truth is, I don't. I've got no way to pay you."

They exchanged glances and one of them, David Kenner,

asked, "Would you be willing to take a polygraph test? Don't get me wrong; I believe you're broke, but if you were to pass a lie detector test, I could submit it to your judge and request that he lower your bail. If you don't have any money, you're less of a flight risk."

I shrugged. "Fine with me."

"Good. I'll set it up for tomorrow," he added.

❖ ❖ ❖

Over the next few weeks, David Kenner visited me daily. The polygraph results were filed in district court. The media picked up on the motion and reported that "an independent polygraph examination revealed that Barry Minkow has no assets—hidden or otherwise."

To better acquaint himself with the case, David had me write a detailed, chronological outline of events from October 1982 to July 1987. This project kept me very busy, so time passed quickly.

David's associate had a full schedule and was unable to continue representing me, but David assured me he was quite capable of handling the case alone. Though we couldn't persuade Judge Tevrizian to set a lower bail, David convinced the prison lieutenant to drop the escape investigation. Yet because of the high publicity of my case, I was kept in the hole.

The best thing about David Kenner was his support for and belief in my conversion to Christianity. Even though he himself wasn't a Christian, he *never* doubted the authenticity of my faith, nor did he label me a "born-again-until-you're-out-again" Christian.

❖ ❖ ❖

As the days passed, I continued to adjust to my new environment. It wasn't easy learning how to respond to so many different responsibilities. In fact, my response once almost cost me my life.

I was being led back from a visit with Kenner while still in the hole. Another inmate had poked his head through his cell's trapdoor and said, "Hey, Minkow, nice tennis shoes. Can I have 'em?"

Thinking he was kidding, I turned and said, "Sure."

A few minutes later an inmate orderly came to my cell to pick up the shoes. When I told him I'd just been kidding, he went off to relay that message.

Five minutes later he was back. "You're dead, Minkow! That dude says he's gonna kill you!"

"He wants to kill me over a pair of tennis shoes?"

"The guy thinks you don't respect him. You promised him the shoes in front of everyone, and now you're backing out. For that he'll kill you. That's how it works in the joint."

"He may *try* to kill me," I said, drawing myself up proudly. Though I'd been off steroids for months, I still had some muscle size.

My new roommate, a bank robber who'd been in prison twice before, tried to warn me. "You know, Barry, I've seen too many guys die over ridiculous things like TV shows and tennis shoes." Then, to prove he was taking the threat seriously, he put up a sign with an arrow pointing to my bunk: "Barry Minkow is on the top bunk."

That night I could barely sleep. I jumped every time I heard a sound. If the guy were already doing a life sentence, killing me wouldn't make any difference to him. Was a fifty-dollar pair of tennis shoes worth my life?

The next morning I called the orderly over. "Hey, buddy, do me a favor and give the guy these shoes."

The next day, as I was being escorted to another visit with David Kenner, I saw the "tennis shoe man" in the corner of the waiting area. Having only seen his head through the trapdoor, I was surprised to find that the guy was a lot bigger than I'd imagined. He was wearing my shoes.

"Mr. Z-Best . . . how're ya doing?" he asked.

"I'm all right."

He stood up straight and walked right up to me. "Listen, man," he said, "I've been in this system a long time and I've got even longer to go. And I want to give you some advice, because it looks like you're going to spend some time with the Feds." He put his hand on my shoulder and stared directly into my eyes. "I don't care who you were on the streets and how many people you conned in the past. What's done is done! When you come to prison, you've got a fresh start. With real convicts, your word is your bond. No one judges you for who you used to be—only for who you are right now." He stepped back and surveyed his feet. "I appreciate the shoes, man. They'll probably last me five years."

"No problem!" I said. "Your advice is going to stay with me a lot longer than that."

❖ ❖ ❖

The trial began in late August of 1988. The biggest concern Kenner and I had were the forty-eight witnesses the government had ready to testify against me. I had burned so many bridges behind me that there was no way of knowing how they would testify.

Judge Tevrizian opposed the idea of a long, drawn-out trial. But my ego once again got in the way. I was angered because I was being blamed for everything. Fuller, Robbins, Cox, and others had made lots of money off me and were free, while I faced a fifty-four-count indictment. It wasn't fair! I couldn't cooperate with the government against my former associates, but I could do whatever I had to in my own defense. And that's exactly what I did. In the trial, I claimed that the people behind the scenes forced me—as a puppet—to commit the crimes during my reign at ZZZZ Best.

It took the government more than two months to present its case. They brought two surprise witnesses—including Mike McGee as well as another close friend. The hardest part of my fall came when I listened to these men, whom I loved so dearly, turn against me. But I deserved it. While it was happening, my dad comforted me and Mom told me, "Barry, when you plant onions in your garden, don't cry when onions come up." My friends weren't to blame—I was. The lies, cons, and manipulations I had once sown were now being "reaped" in a humiliating public trial. The press was in the courtroom every day, reporting on each new event.

When the government rested its case, Judge Tevrizian shocked everyone by offering me a "special" deal. In conference with David Kenner he offered me twelve years if I would plead guilty and end the trial. If it continued, I would have to face the music—perhaps a much stiffer sentence.

I was given the weekend to decide.

Gladiator School | 17

M r. Minkow, I'm holding in my hand a copy of an indictment which alleges that you were involved in a massive scheme to defraud banks, investors, Wall Street, and the IRS. Are you guilty of these offenses?" Mr. Kenner asked me from a podium in Judge Tevrizian's courtroom.

"I am," I responded in a soft, low tone. The courtroom spectators groaned.

"Can you please tell the ladies and gentlemen of the jury *why* you committed these offenses; that is, were you under duress when you did these things?" he continued, taking off his glasses.

"Yes! I was afraid I'd be physically harmed if I didn't."

I had rejected the judge's offer and continued with the trial because of my insatiable need for love and acceptance. For more than two months, the government had stopped at nothing to portray me as the worst liar in the history of American business. Had I taken the judge's deal and pled guilty, I would have confessed to everything that had been said about me. I just couldn't stop worrying about the opinion of "others." Thus, I put my relationship with Jesus (now well over a year old) on the back burner and lied under oath to avoid prison and impress the public.

But something went terribly wrong during my testimony. My once enthusiastic and convincing presence was undercut by strong feelings of guilt, by uncharacteristically slow and plodding responses. I was on the stand for nearly a week, and each day I became less and less believable. When I finally finished, I knew I had made the biggest mistake of my life. I lay in my dark cell, asking myself what went wrong. Why was I so unconvincing? For years I had put on great performances when it counted; yet when my life was on the line, I had failed.

No one seemed more disappointed with my decision to testify than Judge Dickran Tevrizian. He had offered me the opportunity for a lighter sentence and a chance to rehabilitate myself in prison.

The jury was out three and one-half days—short for a four-and-one-half-month trial—and returned to a courtroom filled with media waiting to see if Barry Minkow had pulled off his final con. The judge told me to stand. All eyes were on me—except those of the jurors. They wouldn't look at me. David Kenner had warned me earlier, "If they don't look at you, it's because they're ashamed, because they found you guilty." My palms began to sweat.

The jury foreman began to speak: "We, the jury, find the defendant, Barry Minkow, *guilty* of Count 1, Count 2, Count 3 . . ." all the way to Count 57 (the government had added three counts in a superseding indictment)!

I should have taken the judge's deal, I thought. My pride had buried me again.

After the verdict, the marshals hustled me to the holding cell to await my trip back to prison. The judge allowed me one phone call.

I called my family. "Dad, is that you?"

"Yeah, Barry, it's me. Did they reach a verdict yet?"

"They found me guilty on all counts." I began to cry.

"That's all right, Barry. Your Mom and I love you and will help you make it through this," he assured me.

"Thanks, Dad," I said, choking on my tears. "I've got to go now."

When I hung up, I sat and thought about the four-and-one-half-month trial. I faced a potential 285 years in prison, and the reputation my ego had fought so hard to protect was ruined forever. With everything looking hopeless, I sat alone in my cell and prayed. I wondered if even Jesus could forgive me for all I had done. *At least forgiveness is something I now care about,* I said to myself.

❖   ❖   ❖

After the trial, I was moved from Terminal Island to the Metropolitan Detention Center in downtown Los Angeles where I was taken out of the hole and placed among the general population. Surprisingly, many of my fellow inmates there provided tremendous encouragement, which gave me something I hadn't had since July of 1987—namely, hope. Though Christmas was only weeks away and I was facing a long prison sentence, I began to realize that my life wasn't over. With the trial behind me, I could now begin repairing my life.

The media wouldn't let it rest, though. Newspapers across the country continued to beat the drums about the heinous Barry Minkow. Some even likened me to Adolf Hitler. One night, I fulfilled my dream of making it onto "The Tonight Show," albeit ignominiously. Carson joked during his monologue about my writing a Christmas card to my mother, telling her I'd be home for Christmas in the year 2049! I was paying a heavy price for all the trouble I'd caused.

Sentencing was scheduled for late March 1989. To keep busy until then, I volunteered to work in the bakery, rising at 3:45 A.M. and finishing at noon. I spent the rest of the day reading my Bible and working out. I enjoyed getting my body back in shape—this time without steroids! My family visited once a week, and Donna came at least twice a month. I figured it was only a matter of time before she left me, and I couldn't blame her. She had found out about Brenda, Susan, and all the others, and she was too young to wait ten or twenty years for me. But that didn't dull the pain.

These consequences are killers, I said to myself.

With Maggie shut away in a convalescent hospital, I missed having someone in my life who could counsel me with my problems and explain the Bible to me. One day, while listening to the radio in my cell, the enthusiastic voice and confident teaching style of a Bible teacher caught my attention. He had a unique way of practically applying the teachings of the Bible. I wrote him a letter, and he wrote me back. In fact, since he lived in Southern California, he even visited a Bible study group I had started that met every night between 7:30 and 8:00.

Some inmates doubted my "new" desire to hold Bible studies and go to church, and ridiculed me for it. "Reading that Bible ain't going to get you out of prison," they would say, or "Why didn't you go to church when you were stealing all those millions on the street?" Others thought I was trying to score points with the judge before sentencing.

These objections were answered on sentencing day—March 29, 1989—before a courtroom filled with the media, past victims, and curious bystanders, all anxious to see the gavel fall on Barry Minkow. Yet, despite the humiliation and embarrassment, I had a certain peace within my heart, an assurance that somehow things would be okay. My only worry was for my mom, sitting in the third row. Would she break down and cry? Would she ever get over seeing her son sentenced to years in prison? Such questions flooded my mind as I spoke my piece before sentence was imposed. After apologizing for my crimes, I made an unusual statement: "Your Honor, to prove to you that I have accepted responsibility for my actions, I am hereby waiving my right to appeal the conviction. I've wasted enough of this court's time."

Judge Tevrizian appeared skeptical of my sudden change of

heart; he reminded me that I had ten days after the sentencing to file a notice of appeal. Then dead silence fell on the courtroom. *It's consequences time,* I said to myself. The judge sentenced me to twenty-five years in prison and twenty-six million dollars in restitution. The spectators were shocked at the severity of the sentence.

As the marshals rushed me out of the courtroom, with the press descending on me, hoping for a juicy quote for the evening news, I looked back at my mother. The twenty-five years was bad, but I could handle it as long as Mom was going to be okay. When my eyes met hers, she smiled, nodded, and pointed upward. I read her lips: "It'll be okay. . . . It'll be okay. . . ." I'll never forget that day—my once nervous and unstable mother sitting there with the confidence and serenity of a deep and abiding faith in the living God and encouraging her son as he was hauled away to prison for twenty-five years.

That evening the largest crowd ever showed up for my Bible study. TV news had informed everyone of my long sentence and the twenty-six-million-dollar fine. Before the study began, a friend I had met in prison came to my room and told me I didn't have to show up if I didn't want to. "This is my chance to prove that my commitment to Christ is for real," I told him.

Before he left my room, he grabbed my arm and asked, "Are you really going to waive your right to appeal after a four-and-a-half-month trial?"

"Well, I'm guilty and it's time I took responsibility for what I've done. You know, buddy, it's never too late to start doing what's right."

I was nervous when I began speaking to the group that evening, but the more I opened up, the easier it became. I gave a short testimony about my experiences over the past six and one-half years, beginning with my steroid abuse and working my way forward.

"'As long as I can bench-press four hundred pounds *now,*

who cares about the future?' I would always say." Many in the group had taken steroids in the past—to make the high school football team or to enhance their physiques. They understood what I meant when I said, "I was willing to risk my *future* health for some temporary glory."

But many hadn't, so I brought up a subject that was universally understood: *money.* I explained why the risk of prison never discouraged me from committing crimes: "I wanted to be rich and famous *now.* . . . Who cared about the future as long as I was driving a Ferrari!"

The highlight of that evening came when I confessed my "hidden agenda" for becoming a Christian. I told the group that the only reason I had originally accepted Christ was to, hopefully, avoid going to prison. "But God took my wrong motives and accepted me despite my manipulative personality."

When I concluded my talk, several men thanked me for being honest. Some admitted their original skepticism and were convinced that I was at last on the right track. I went back to my room, lay on my bunk, and thought about how good it had felt to be honest with people. But then I remembered the twenty-five-year sentence. In a matter of weeks the Bureau of Prisons would redesignate me to another institution to complete that long sentence. I worried that it would be too far from home or too violent.

❖   ❖   ❖

"Englewood, Colorado," said my case manager. "That's where you will be serving your sentence, Mr. Minkow."

"But that's twelve hundred miles from home!" I argued. "My family can't afford to fly all the way to Colorado to visit me."

"You should have thought about that before you took Wall

Street to the cleaners. . . . Now get out of my office!" he said sternly.

I walked out, dejected and confused. No one else in my case had been sent outside California. Then again, no one in my case had received a twenty-five-year sentence. Carl Stowe and Gary Todd were given nine years each; Jerry Williams, one year. While they would serve their time in California-based prison camps, I was on my way to a prison many had nicknamed the "Gladiator School."

Discouraged, I went back to my room and picked up my mail. Roberta Clancy, a friend for several years, had sent a brochure and catalog on Liberty University. Aware of my conversion to Christianity, she had encouraged me on the phone a few days earlier to make the best of my situation and earn a degree from a fully accredited four-year college, specifically, a Christian college. She had even offered to help finance my education, which was amazing because she had lost a good deal of money in ZZZZ Best stock.

As I glanced through the catalog, I was instantly impressed with their videotape/external degree program. The thought of earning a bachelor's degree from start to finish appealed to me. Throughout my life, I had never accomplished anything honestly. Completing a legitimate college education would change that. Of course, I didn't know if I would have access to a video player in the Colorado prison. But if I were serious about my Christian faith, I could trust the Lord to open the doors for me. I didn't need to "manipulate" the situation, as in times past.

Within weeks, I was on Con-Air, a special fleet of planes that transports federal prisoners around the country. The two-hour trip from California to Colorado, with my hands cuffed and my legs shackled, seemed like an eternity. We landed and boarded a heavily guarded bus bound for the Federal Correctional Institution in Englewood, Colorado. As we approached this massive prison complex, I saw the guard towers and razor wire snaking along both an inner and outer fence. This looked like a very tough place.

At orientation, where staff members explained how the institution functions, I was particularly impressed by the warden. "How many of you are from California?" he asked. Many of us raised our hands. "That's almost 90 percent of you. Let me first say that because the prison system is overcrowded, there will be no transfers back to California. So, don't even ask." As I surveyed the room, I noticed that I wasn't the only one discouraged by this news.

"My next question is: How many of you have filed an appeal?" Most in the room raised their hands. I did not. "Good. And I hope you all win and go home to your families soon. But unfortunately, as you know, only a small percentage of you will actually win your appeals. So, let me give you some good advice . . . unpack! We've got plenty of programs here to keep you busy. We have an education department, two weight rooms, trade schools, and various church programs, depending on your beliefs. So, think about what you most enjoy doing and get started. Otherwise, your time here will seem like forever."

Unpack! Don't live day to day expecting to be released. Start over and get a life. *That's exactly what I need to do,* I thought. Instead of feeling sorry for myself, I was going to use this opportunity to turn my life around.

I went to the Education Department and met with Ramona Nelson who was in charge of my housing unit. I described the program offered by Liberty University, explaining the requirements for a video player and a person to administer exams. She reviewed the school's brochure and authorized Liberty University to send me the books, tapes, and other materials.

When I got back to the unit, I called Roberta Clancy and told her that the prison would allow me to go ahead with the video program. "My only problem now is the money," I said to her.

"Call me back in half an hour," she replied. "I'm going to call the school and arrange the financing for you."

While I waited, I prayed and asked God for His assistance: *Lord, this is the first honest endeavor I've ever been involved in. Please help Roberta set up some kind of financing for me.*

It took less than thirty minutes for God to answer my prayer. When I called Roberta back, everything was done. Through government Pell grants and guaranteed student loans, she had arranged for me to begin my education immediately. *I love this FCI Englewood,* I said to myself as I hung up the phone.

❖ ❖ ❖

In August of 1989, while working in the bakery, I was summoned to Ramona Nelson's office. She told me that her education supervisor had canceled my video schooling because it "wasn't a program that they could let every inmate participate in." I sat there in her office, shocked at the news. Here I was, trying to rehabilitate myself and being stopped cold.

When I regained my composure, I went to see the supervisor. She invited me into her office and listened attentively as I made my case for the video program. But, in the end, she stood by her decision.

Rather than argue with her, I left the office, disappointed, defeated, and ready to throw in the towel. *Is this my reward for trying to change?* I asked God. I was beginning to realize that my past involvement with ZZZZ Best wasn't going to be easily forgotten.

❖ ❖ ❖

"Don't give up," Jeff Lawson said to me as we sat together in my tiny room. "If the Lord wants Barry Minkow to get an education, no one will be able to stop it!"

Jeff, in prison for over ten years, was one of the first people I met at Englewood. He had a number of tattoos and he feared no one. He was also a Christian who had the respect of everyone because he "walked his talk."

"Why should I even bother, Jeff?" I sighed. "No matter how hard I try, no one is ever going to believe I've changed."

"There you go, feeling sorry for yourself. You're nothing but a crybaby! Just because some cop gave you a hard time, you're ready to quit Christianity. And that's what your problem's been throughout your life. You're a quitter, Barry, a quitter! When things get tough, you either quit or take a shortcut."

So much for the "loving brother" approach. But Jeff was right: I needed a good dose of reality. I was a quitter who took shortcuts whenever life or business threw me a curve.

"So, what should I do?" I asked him.

"Two things: Start praying, and talk to the warden."

So that's what I did. The next day I saw the warden in the dining room during the noon meal. He listened attentively to my problem and promised to look into it.

That night I reported this news to Jeff in his room. On his locker was a picture of a biker wearing a T-shirt that read: I'M A SINNER SAVED BY GRACE . . . WHAT KIND OF SINNER ARE YOU?

"Good, Barry. I'm proud of you," he said. "By the way, I was thinking about what you said to me yesterday about people never forgetting about the ZZZZ Best deal, and I have a suggestion for you."

"What?"

"Have you ever apologized to all those people you stole money from?"

I thought about this question. Embarrassment and pride had kept me from contacting past victims. "No, I haven't," I admitted.

"Then that's your next project. Have those fancy lawyers of

yours get the addresses of as many victims as they can. Then write them all letters explaining that you're sorry for what you did to them."

"What if they don't believe me?"

"Who cares? The Lord will honor the effort. He knows what's in your heart."

"That's what scares me," I muttered under my breath.

❖   ❖   ❖

A week later Ramona Nelson informed me that the warden had overruled the education supervisor's decision; I would be able to continue my education—indefinitely. I also wrote my victims letters of apology, almost fifty of them. Unfortunately, one of my letters to a Wall Street executive was leaked to the press. In November 1989, *USA Today* detailed my "alleged remorse from prison."

With permission to continue my Liberty education, I studied seven days a week, became actively involved in the Christian programs at the chapel, and of course, continued to lift weights. Slowly but surely, the staff members stopped seeing me as Barry Minkow, the con man, and began seeing me as someone striving for change. The person who encouraged me the most during this transition period was a woman who worked in the Education Department and proctored most of my Liberty University exams. She believed in me—even when her boss didn't. She kept me disciplined and insisted that I put in my study time.

Once she even summoned me from the weight room over the loudspeaker: "You haven't put your hours in today, Mr. Minkow. Now get back to school!"

The inmates laughed at me and mimicked her words. But it was this kind of accountability I desperately needed. And it paid off. At the end of my first semester, I made the dean's list with a 3.6 GPA.

❖ ❖ ❖

I also learned why FCI Englewood was called the "Gladiator School." Although it was not as violent as some of the penitentiaries, several of its inmates had committed murder and other violent crimes. There were plenty of fights, a few food strikes, and lots of intimidation.

In prison a man must *earn* credibility and respect. No one liked phonies, and all were skeptical of inmates who, like me, embraced "religion" as part of their daily routines. In an odd sort of way, prison actually resembled Wall Street. A public company that was *consistently* profitable year in and year out was recommended as a "good buy" by analysts and experts. In like manner, an inmate who *said* he was a Christian and *acted* like one was labeled "good people" by his fellow prisoners. When you eat, sleep, weight-lift, study, worship, and play sports with 850 men in a confined area, it doesn't take them long to discover what kind of person you *really* are. And when they find out, word spreads fast.

My big test came in the annual East Side versus West Side football game. FCI Englewood was divided between upper and lower east-side units and upper and lower west-side units, and there was a great deal of competition among the units.

I was surprised at how many inmates invited me to play. Although I had played some pickup football games in my youth, I had never played organized football and feared getting into a tackle football game, *in prison,* without pads! But not wanting to appear cowardly, I agreed.

The sidelines were flooded with spectators. Some had come for the violence. Others wanted to support their units. Still others, I later found out, showed up to see if Barry Minkow, the once famous stock-swindler-turned-Christian, could take a hit.

The field was eighty yards long and forty yards wide. Two men from each unit officiated, and each team had a coach. As

I looked at the size of the players, I reevaluated my motives for playing. *Am I trying to please people again?* I thought. Before I could talk myself out of playing, the game began.

The West Side had most of the talent. They jumped to an early lead as I waited on the sidelines to play. I had told our team captain before the game that I wanted to play quarterback. After about twenty minutes, I was called in. *Get me through this one, Lord, and I promise I'll never touch another carpet as long as I live,* I prayed as I jogged out to the field, knowing I was about to get hit hard.

The first play I called was a screen pass to the right. The linemen were to let the defense through and then go out and block for the pass receiver. Unfortunately, the receiver went too deep, and I was faced with a heavy rush. I was chased to the right by a pack of hard-charging linemen and, too scared to stop and throw the ball, continued down the sideline until two linebackers and a safety caught up to me. To avoid contact, I stepped out of bounds, but that didn't stop my pursuers. They hit me so hard I flew five feet into the stands. I could hear the oohs and ahhs from the spectators as I popped up and made my way back to the field.

"At least we got the first down," I said to the men in the huddle, brushing pebbles, gravel, and grass off my arms and legs.

Next, I called a simple out-pattern to the tight end on the left side. "Ready . . . set . . . hike." I had to jump for the snap and when I looked for my receiver, he was covered. I rolled left and looked for another receiver. The rush was breaking through the line. With my head still ringing from the last hit, I tucked the ball under my arm and sprinted down the left sideline. The crowd roared when they saw I might go all the way. But just when I thought I was home free, two guys sacrificed their bodies, diving and sideswiping me into the crowd. I popped up again, but this time in extreme slow motion.

"Not as easy as Wall Street, is it, Minkow?" said one of the guys who had hit me.

My body ached, my face was a gravel mosaic, and I knew then and there why so many guys had asked me to play—they were gunning for me! I wanted to quit. But then I saw Jeff Lawson staring at me from the sidelines. Somehow he knew what I was thinking. I went back to the huddle.

The rest of the game proved to be more of the same. In fact, there were so many injuries that the recreation supervisor thereafter prohibited any tackle football. When it was over, the West Side had beaten us, but not by much. Although I had thrown a couple interceptions, I had gained the respect of several of my critics by hanging in there. As I limped back to the unit, many of the men came up and congratulated me.

I couldn't help but see the irony. Just two and a half years earlier, I had been the respected president of a public company. Now I was fighting to earn credibility through a tackle football game in a federal prison.

❖ ❖ ❖

During my second year at FCI Englewood, I helped make a video on fraud prevention. A friend had told me about a nonprofit organization in Austin, Texas, that trained accountants and other professionals to detect and prevent fraud. I wrote a letter to the chairman and explained my desire to assist in any way I could. I was surprised when he asked that I do a videotaped interview in which I would disclose the techniques used at ZZZZ Best to con accountants and other professionals.

I wanted to help the organization and believed it was the right thing to do, but I was concerned that such a video might be misinterpreted by the public or my fellow inmates. Prisoners who cooperate with the government or other authorities are ridiculed and often threatened. The worst reputation to have while in custody is that of "rat" or "snitch." If I did this video and the other inmates found out, I could have some serious problems.

Two things helped me overcome this obstacle. First, I was not asked any questions relating to others' involvement in ZZZZ Best—especially those who were never indicted.

Second, I got some good advice from a great Christian friend, James Long. When Jeff Lawson left, James became my new closest friend. We shared a room and played on the same flag-football team. His nickname was "Peanut," but he was anything but small. He could bench-press about 450 pounds and had a bodybuilder's physique. Peanut had earned the respect of both staff members and inmates because, though he was black, he loved everyone, without any prejudice. He told me, "You can't run away from the opposition. . . . You can't hide under your bunk for the rest of your life, afraid of what others *might* say about you. Take the opposition head-on and fear nothing. If God is with you, no one can stop you." Fueled by those words, I agreed to do the video.

❖　❖　❖

"Hey, Mom, it's Barry. How's Maggie?" I asked.

Mom was glad to hear from me, but her tone sobered when she answered my question about Maggie. "The same. She's still in the convalescent hospital, and she still can't talk."

"Did she get my last letter?"

"Yes, and she's very proud of you. I visited her a couple of days ago, and when she read your letter about doing the fraud-prevention video, she cried."

"Do me a favor, Mom. Go see her and tell her that I'm coming back from the ZZZZ Best fall . . . because it's never too late to start doing what's right!"

My one concern with doing the nationally-released video was that I not come across as if I were bragging or boasting about my past crimes. With a stage under my feet and an audience in front of me, my ego had usually turned whatever I was doing into "The Barry Minkow Show."

The night before the show, Peanut advised me: "Whenever you feel like bragging, just think of a victim who was hurt by your crime. Picture that person in your mind, and that'll keep you in check."

I thought about Pat Chapman and his huge loss. His words before he gave me the money echoed in my head: "I trust you, Barry." With that in mind, I was ready for the interview.

Much to my surprise, the interviewer sought academic rather than personal information. This format kept me in check throughout the taping. When it was over, I ran back to my room and told Peanut how much his advice had helped me. "I think there's hope for you, yet," he joked.

After the video, I was asked to participate in fraud seminars, answering questions from accountants and lawyers across the country by telephone. One man asked if this was another "Barry Minkow con," or if I was serious about helping others and changing my ways. It was a fair question and one that deserved an answer. "From an economic standpoint, it's far more profitable for me to pursue a career in fraud *prevention* than it is to pursue a career in fraud *perpetration*," I told him. "And, believe me, it's a lot less risky!" The audience laughed at the response, but it made sense. I wasn't forcing the public to believe me because I had converted to Christ and was now sincere; I was defending my turnaround in common-sense terms even skeptics could not dispute.

My involvement with fraud prevention greatly increased my confidence for comeback. Society often shuns men in prison and tells them they have nothing positive to offer. Indeed, many of my fellow inmates at Englewood chose to simply give up, not even attempting rehabilitation. They had been classically conditioned to believe the old saying, "Once a crook, always a crook." Other former criminals and I challenged this misconception as we were used to help the very people we had once hurt.

In March 1991 the *Wall Street Journal* ran a front-page story about my involvement with the National Association of Certified Fraud Examiners. Some of the inmates were angered that I had publicly disclosed my "tricks of the trade." And even though I didn't mention anyone by name, some viewed it as a betrayal of the inmate code.

Three days after the article came out, I was buying supplies at the inmate commissary. A clerk in the store began to ridicule me for the video, saying I was probably hurting some guy out in the world who was pulling off a scam—by training people how to catch him. I told him I wished my fraud had been detected before I completed the public stock offering, because if it had been, I wouldn't still be in jail. "Sometimes we need to be protected from ourselves," I said.

"Why don't you just become a cop, Barry?" he shot back.

The other inmates in the commissary became very quiet. *Cop* was a fighting word in prison society; call someone a cop and expect an altercation.

"Look, pal," I said angrily, "I'm going to pretend I didn't

hear that. But just for the record, I didn't do this video to win your approval!"

"Yeah, you did it for the money!"

"That's where you're wrong, my friend. I didn't receive one dime for that video." I paused to allow the onlookers to digest this information. "Now, maybe *you* want to go right back out into the real world and continue a career in fraud, but don't put me in that car—I'm out for good!"

A friend who saw I wasn't getting anywhere pulled me aside. "Come on, Barry, he's just jealous because he ain't doing nothing to help nobody but himself."

That night in my bunk, I realized this was just the beginning. The more I tried to improve myself, the more resistance I would encounter. But thanks to friends like Jeff Lawson and Peanut, I decided that no matter what the consequences, I wasn't going to quit. And I didn't!

❖   ❖   ❖

"Barry, I have to go to my office to make a phone call. Just keep working on the test, and I'll be back in fifteen minutes," the proctor said as she left the general education room.

It was lunchtime and I was taking my Liberty math final. As I stared down at the 100-question test, I remembered that Shaun Redgate, my academic advisor at Liberty University, had told me that if I wanted to stay on the dean's list, I needed a B or better on this exam. Math was difficult for me; I had a D average in the class. The longer I pored over the exam, the more I became convinced I could never get a B on this test.

I looked at the proctor's desk in the front of the room. My notes were in the top drawer. *If I could get my hands on those notes for about ten minutes, I could ace this test!* I thought. If I didn't, I'd end up with a D in the class. Faced with the possibility of failure, I went to the door and looked down the hall to make sure the proctor was still on the phone. I rushed over to the desk, ready to pull open the top drawer and review the notes. But then it hit me.

I thought about Maggie Clay, Jeff Lawson, and Peanut. *You're a quitter, Barry—always looking for a shortcut.* I thought about the fraud video and the commissary clerk. My hands began to sweat. I needed to act quickly. I thought back to Ron's Convenience Store. My decision there had marked the beginning of my criminal career. I thought about the guys in prison who doubted the authenticity of my Christian conversion. *I'd be confirming their claims,* I said to myself. But then I thought about the embarrassment of a D on my record, and removal from the dean's list. *No one will ever know. And I'll never do it again.* I moved closer to the desk and reached for the drawer . . . but stopped. *God will know . . . and there's no conning Him.* I backed away from the desk and sat down in my chair.

Five minutes later, the test supervisor came back. "How's it going?" she asked.

I grimaced. "Not great, but I'm trying."

A week later Shaun Redgate told me I had failed the final and was receiving a D in the class.

❖ ❖ ❖

The church activities at FCI Englewood played a major role in my life. Several outside volunteer groups, including Prison Fellowship, Residents Encounter Christ, and Koinonia, met weekly in the chapel area and offered inmates a forum to share their deepest concerns with caring volunteers. During my third year at Englewood, I was chosen president of one of these groups—the Fellowship of Christian Athletes. I organized athletic events, lined up speakers for our weekly meetings, and encouraged participation among the inmates. Because this was my first official leadership position since the collapse of ZZZZ

Best, I was afraid. But with the assistance of several friends and a great staff chaplain, I succeeded.

I also finished my bachelor of science degree in church ministries. I wanted to work on a master's degree through Liberty's video correspondence program, but with money scarce and a D on my undergraduate transcripts, I doubted that it would be possible.

I had changed jobs and was working at the UNICOR factory, assembling radio mounts for the M-1 tank. My boss was an older man who had taken a liking to me. When I explained my problem to him, he suggested that I apply for a special UNICOR scholarship grant offered to factory employees, and I was approved for a partial scholarship.

Then I called Shaun Redgate to probe other ways of financing the balance of the program. "Look, Shaun, I know I've got a D on my record, but math is a tough subject for me. Do you think you can still accept me into the master's program?"

"Of course we'll accept you. Even with the D, you still have better than a 3.0 average . . . no problem."

"Well, the money is a problem," I added. "Because Pell grants can't be used for graduate school, I'm stuck."

"What about the money you're earning in UNICOR?"

"Fifty percent of whatever I make goes to the victims of my crimes," I explained. "That doesn't leave me with much to live on."

"Are you kidding? You're really making payments to the victims of ZZZZ Best? How much have you paid so far?"

"Almost four thousand dollars."

"All from what you earned in prison?"

"Every penny."

"Well, that's impressive!" He paused. "Let me see what I can do for you. Call me back tomorrow."

When I called back, Shaun told me that Liberty University

was granting me a five-thousand-dollar scholarship. I began working on my master's degree immediately.

❖ ❖ ❖

After more than three years at medium-security FCI Englewood, I was moved to the minimum-security camp directly across the street. As I walked out the steel gates, I thought about the friends I was leaving behind and wondered if they would remember me. There was something special about spending four Christmas seasons away from home with the same bunch of guys. I turned around and took one last look at the place where my comeback had begun.

The camp proved to be an entirely different environment from the FCI. There was far less violence, and the majority of the men were serving shorter sentences, primarily for nonviolent crimes.

During my six-month stay at FPC (Federal Prison Camp) Englewood, I continued my graduate-level studies and was chosen to work on a special suicide-prevention team. A program had been developed wherein prisoners assisted recently committed inmates who had attempted or had threatened to commit suicide. These men were placed in a single cell, much like the one I had lived in at Terminal Island. A suicide-prevention team member, working in four-hour shifts around the clock, would sit in front of the cell and talk with the person in need.

I was glad to be part of this program because I remembered how I had contemplated suicide back in Terminal Island, when I'd faced over 250 years in prison. There was, however, one restriction, of which the staff psychologist constantly reminded me: "No preaching! You're there to *comfort* them, Barry—not *convert* them." But I didn't listen to her. How could I possibly help someone in the same position I had once been in without telling him about Jesus? I'll never forget the first man I watched.

He was angry at the world and wanted to kill everyone—even me. He cussed at me, called me names, and even told the psychologist that I had tried to give him a Bible (which I had).

I prayed for the man and asked God to soften his heart. A day or two later, while I was at work in the kitchen, the chaplain told me that the man in the suicide cell had asked to see him. They talked for several hours and afterwards the inmate said a prayer, asking Jesus to come into his life. "We're a good team, Barry," he said. I smiled.

❖ ❖ ❖

During my short stay at the Englewood camp, I met two Christian men in their mid-forties who loved reading and studying the Bible. When they learned that I had a degree in church ministries and was working on my master's, they encouraged me to teach a Christian evidences class for the men at the camp. At first I was apprehensive, fearing opposition and criticism. But they pointed out that I should expect a tremendous amount of ridicule and rejection when I got out of prison.

"You need to prepare yourself for criticism, Barry," one of them told me. "Anyone who tries to come back from failure and turn his life around must endure persecution. So get used to it now!"

I followed their advice and taught a ten-week class designed to demonstrate that Christianity is a system of belief based on good reason and not blind faith. I used textbooks and videos to emphasize key points. It was a great experience because it taught me two very important things: I discovered how much I enjoyed teaching people about the Bible and I learned not to overreact when other inmates hurled insults at me such as, "Hey, look. It's Barry Bakker's class!" or "You guys better watch out for Fleece the Flock Minkow!" Anticipating ridicule helped prepare me to deal with it.

By the end of 1992, I had earned a master of arts degree in religion. Shaun Redgate was so impressed with how quickly I had finished the program that he encouraged me to pursue further education. He recommended me to the University of South Africa because they had a well-respected systematic theology department. I immediately applied to their master's doctoral program.

❖ ❖ ❖

I was nearing the end of my fifth year in custody. (That was more than Michael Milken and Ivan Boesky combined!) The parole board had told me in March of 1992 that I would have to serve nine years before I could be paroled. They were, however, impressed with my educational accomplishments and exhorted me to "keep up the good work and come back in two years." Although I determined not to let this nine-year date discourage me, I did say one prayer over and over again: "Lord, please give me one more chance and I won't let You down—just one more chance."

On December 28, 1992, I was transferred from FPC Englewood to FPC Lompoc in California. I had asked for the transfer because I wanted to be closer to my father, who had suffered a stroke.

At Lompoc, I continued to prepare myself for the University of South Africa by researching topics for my prospective dissertation. I also worked out daily and taught a class on Christian evidences every Tuesday night. I held two jobs simultaneously: one in the bakery, which meant getting up at 3:00 A.M. Monday through Friday, and the other as chaplain's clerk, helping organize chapel programs at the camp.

It took some time to adjust to the inmates at Lompoc. At FCI Englewood, those who were hurting emotionally sought out the help of others. But many of the men at Lompoc were professional people—lawyers, accountants, bankers, doctors—who never dreamed they would one day end up in a federal prison. They were embarrassed by their incarceration and, because of pride, maintained a certain distance from others, attempting to fight the battle of loneliness and depression by themselves.

One day I noticed a man of about forty, totally preoccupied with a small, blond child who appeared to be around seven years of age. She was obviously his daughter, but they displayed a love for one another that I had never seen before. When they played together, she never left his side. If he was in the snack area buying a cold drink, she was right there next to him. Together, the two of them had not a care in the world—until it was time to part. Then they hugged for almost five minutes. When the little girl's aunt walked her to the parking lot, the child walked backwards, waving and locking her eyes on her dad's—both sets of eyes welling with tears as the reality of separation set in.

A few days later, I encountered the man in the mail line. After introducing himself as Reid, he said, "I was in church last week and listened to your sermon. I've been listening to some of the radio ministries, and you're good."

I was surprised and flattered, though I didn't feel I deserved such praise. "Thanks, but I'm not even close to these radio speakers. Besides, many of the guys here think my conversion is just another con."

"So let 'em think it," Reid shot back. "Are you going to concentrate on the people who want to see you fail, or are you going to help the ones who need your message?"

I was surprised at the harshness of his comments, especially considering the fact that I'd just met him. But I could see pain in his face, so I remained silent.

"I had almost everything you had, Barry . . . until a dinner with a bank customer, where I agreed to compromise, cost me everything. This camp is full of once high-powered people who have lost it all, including their wives and children. They're hurting and could use some help."

I waited, not knowing what to say. "Was that your daughter I saw you with this weekend?"

"Yeah," he said finally. "She's six." More silence, and then Reid said, "It's all about consequences, Barry. I'm sure you know that. Anyway, a lot of these corporate guys aren't going to reach out, even though they're hurting. It's someone like you who's going to have to make the first move."

"You're probably right, but I sure get tired of the doubters and the obstacles I encounter, especially after all this time."

"Well, you're probably being prepared for something," Reid replied. "And who do you think is preparing you? God! So don't give up."

I laughed. "Reid, I can see why you were sent here. Paul had his Barnabas, and I have you."

"So be it," he said. "I'm your Barnabas. But I still need help with those consequences."

"Don't we all," I replied.

After that, Reid and I became good friends, talking many hours about our past mistakes and future hopes.

❖ ❖ ❖

"I got your letter—what's the emergency?" I asked the caller, a wife of a friend who was still incarcerated in FCI Englewood.

"It's about Peanut, Barry. . . . He's dead."

"What?" I screamed.

"Two days after he got out of the halfway house, someone shot him. I'm sorry . . ."

I hung up the phone and walked to my chapel office, where I could be alone. Peanut was the best friend I had ever had in my life, and I loved him. As I sat in the chapel room, I remembered the time he had pulled me out of the snow after a flag-football game at Englewood.

It was a big play-off game on a snowy Sunday morning, and

many fans had braved the weather to watch us play. We had the ball on our own five-yard line with only seconds remaining in a zero-zero tie. As quarterback, I called for a short pass play. Peanut objected in the huddle, telling me to put one knee down and allow time to run out and the game to go into overtime. But I didn't listen. I faded back and threw an interception. I dove for the guy right before the goal line, but it was too late. They won. The whole team wanted to sack me—they had played for hours in the cold snow, only to see me throw the game away in the final seconds.

I lay in the snow, facedown, waiting for everyone to leave. When I no longer heard any voices, I raised my head, and there was Peanut.

"You wouldn't listen, would ya?" he said, helping me to my feet. I just kept my head down. "Don't worry, Barry, it's just a game. I still love you and always will!"

Now Peanut was gone. We had planned to open a church together when I got out. He had wanted to be a leader in a church that had an equal balance of black and white members. As I recalled his dream in that chapel office, I made a promise: *Peanut, when I get out, I'm going to open that church we talked about and make you proud of me!*

❖ ❖ ❖

"Well, Mr. Minkow, I see that you have earned a bachelor's degree, a master's degree, and that you are currently working on another master's degree at the University of South Africa. That's very interesting," said the examiner from the United States Parole Commission. "If you'll step out for a few minutes, I'll look over your file and give you a decision."

I left the room and waited outside.

Just give me one more chance, Lord. That's all I ask. I promise I won't let you down.

After nearly seventy-five months in prison, with no disciplinary problems or blemishes on my record, I felt I deserved a break. *Maybe the examiner will take six months off the nine years, leaving me with just over two years to go.* I thought. *Or maybe he'll take off twelve months.* But that was unlikely. The Parole Commission wasn't known for giving large reductions to criminals—especially those with controversial media cases.

Fifteen minutes later I was called back into the office. *No matter what he says or does, I'm still going to press on, Lord,* I prayed.

"I've reviewed your file and must say that it's very impressive. Your involvement with the suicide-prevention team, the schooling, and the classes you teach here all reflect an ability to successfully reenter society. I'm going to move your parole date up *eighteen months,* Mr. Minkow."

A big smile broke out on my face. "Thank you, sir, and you won't be sorry!"

When I left the room, I couldn't wait to tell my class, which would meet that evening at 7:00. Some people in the camp were fond of saying I was only playing the "Christian game" to get a break at the parole board. "Once they give him a reduction, he'll throw his Bible in the garbage!" they said.

But I stood up that night, held up my Bible in front of fifty-five people, and said, "I got a big break from the parole board today, and I'm still holding my Bible tonight! My conversion is no con!"

Afterword

Having come to the end of my story, I ponder the big picture and ask myself, *If I had it to do all over again, what would I do differently?* Indeed, most inmates ask themselves this question at one time or another. For me, it is the question of the ages.

I was deeply marked by an event that took place at FCI Englewood on a cold November day in 1989. Inmates had filled the chapel that day to watch a video created by Dr. Tony Campolo. It was entitled "If You Had It to Do All Over Again, What Would You Do Differently?" The video explores how fifty people over the age of ninety-five answered that question.

As the video lecture began, I was quickly captivated by the three most popular responses:

1. Risk more,
2. Reflect more, and
3. Do more things that will last after you die.

It wasn't "*risk* for the illegal" to which the fifty respondents were referring. They were speaking of a different kind of risk— risk involving an answer to the question that now haunted them most: *What could have been?*

Dr. Campolo explained the difference between *living* and *existing,* and how the former involves taking good, calculated risks while the latter defines the lifestyle of someone trapped by fear. I, on the other hand, was haunted by a different question. Instead of being concerned with *what* could have been, I was plagued with *why* I had risked it all for the almighty dollar.

The second response—"Reflecting more"—was an expression of regret for not stopping and smelling the roses along the way. As the fifty people looked back on their lives, they saw missed opportunities—a baby's first steps, a close friend's wedding, or even enjoying their own birthday party. Time had slipped away without adequate reflection and, as Dr. Campolo so eloquently said, without "the taking in of the moment." The failures of my past are directly related to my inability to *reflect more*.

As I watched Dr. Campolo's video, I was awakened to a simple yet profound fact, one I had never thought of through those troublesome years at ZZZZ Best; namely, that when I died, my titles would die with me. All those fancy titles that I worked (and cheated) so hard for would mean nothing at my death. Like those fifty people, I had wasted too much of my life pursuing a fleeting, empty dream.

At this point in the video lecture, Dr. Campolo introduced the term *testimonies*. According to him, only testimonies live on after one dies. To illustrate this, he told a story about a young boy named Teddy Stallard. I repeat Dr. Campolo's story here because it has had a profound impact on the direction of my life—and has changed it forever.

Teddy's fifth-grade teacher, Mrs. Thompson, never liked him because he was one of those kids who always looked like an unmade bed. His hair was messy, his clothes wrinkled, and he had a musty smell about him. And he seemed to ignore Mrs. Thompson, which offended her. In class, he would just stare off into space and pay no attention to her instruction.

That's why when Teddy turned in his test papers, she took great pleasure in marking, with big red Xs, the incorrect answers; that is, until she ran across the file containing his educational history. It read something like this:

First Grade: Teddy is a good boy with a good attitude but he has some problems at home.

Second Grade: Teddy is a hard worker and a good boy but is deeply troubled. *His mother is terminally ill.*

Third Grade: Teddy is falling way behind. He's totally preoccupied and unresponsive. His mother died this year. His father shows no interest.

Fourth Grade: Teddy is deeply troubled and will flunk without some kind of assistance.

Christmas came and all the kids brought beautifully wrapped gifts to Mrs. Thompson. Much to her surprise, Teddy also brought a gift. It was wrapped in a wrinkled brown paper bag and taped together with Scotch tape. When she opened the gift in front of the class, out fell an old broken bracelet and a half bottle of perfume. Although the class started to laugh, Mrs. Thompson was quick on her feet—she put some perfume on each wrist and held it up for all to smell. The class stopped laughing.

At the end of the day when everyone had left, Teddy Stallard remained behind. He went up to his teacher and said, "Mrs. Thompson, you smell just like my mother did when she wore that perfume, and her bracelet looks nice on you too. I'm glad you liked my gifts." When he walked out of the class, Mrs. Thompson dropped to her knees and prayed for God's forgiveness.

When she returned to school the next day, she was changed. No longer would she be like many other teachers who simply dictated to whomever would listen. Mrs. Thompson decided that she would begin to make a difference in the lives of kids, a difference *that would live on long after she died*. Her conquest began with Teddy. She worked with him after school and provided him with the extra-special attention he so desperately needed. By the end of the year, he was caught up to the rest of the students and prepared to move on.

Several years later, Mrs. Thompson received a letter that read something like this:

Dear Mrs. Thompson,

I'm graduating second in my class and I wanted you to be the first to know.

Love, Teddy Stallard

Four years later she received a second letter that read:

Dear Mrs. Thompson,
I wanted you to be the first to know that I'm graduating first in my class. The university was tough, but I endured.

Love, Teddy

Four years after that, she received another which read:

Dear Mrs. Thompson,
As of today I am Theodore J. Stallard, M.D.—how about that! I'm going to be married on July 27th of this year and I want you to come to the wedding and sit at the table where my mother would have sat. You're the only family I have left now—Dad died last year.

Love, Teddy

Even though I've told this story countless times, I still cry. Perhaps it illustrates what my life lacked in the first twenty-one years. Unlike Mrs. Thompson, I did nothing that would live on after I died. Like helping someone else in a time of need. It was always Barry Minkow first; "my way or the highway."

And I came to find that I wasn't alone. Over the last seven years I've met thousands of people in six different prisons who, like me, look back on their lives and ask, "If I had it to do all over again, what would I have done differently?" In addition to the need to *risk more, reflect more,* and *do more things that would last after they died,* my life story reflects a fourth answer to that question: *Have a saving relationship with Jesus Christ.*

My conversion was not dramatic. I turned my life over to Jesus Christ, not because I broke through some intellectual barrier, but because the old way didn't work! All the fame, fan letters, money, women, and power failed to bring meaning, purpose, and direction to my life.

I recall one man pulling me aside after I had preached a sermon at Lompoc and asking, "Hey, Barry, you're not really serious about this Jesus stuff, are you? Don't you want to get right back out there and make millions again?"

My answer was a simple no, but I clarified myself by adding, "Why would I go right back into a situation that didn't work before? If money and prestige didn't bring peace and contentment to my life the first time around, what makes you think it would now?"

He had no answer. Why? Because when he was free and living a life-style consistent with the money and fame agenda, he knew, deep down, that he wasn't truly happy. When no one else was around, he knew who he *really* was, and with that there is no contentment.

To me, nothing better illustrates the Barry Minkow story than these words written by Malcolm Muggeridge. As a world-renowned journalist, Muggeridge had traveled the globe searching for that one great story, but never found it until he read about Jesus Christ. He writes:

I may, I suppose, regard myself as a relatively successful man. People occasionally stare at me in the streets—that's fame. I can fairly easily earn enough to qualify for admission to the higher slopes of the Internal Revenue—that's success. Furnished with money and a little fame, even the elderly, if they care to, may partake of trendy diversions—that's pleasure. It might happen once in awhile that something I said or wrote was sufficiently heeded for me to persuade myself that it represented a serious impact on our time—that's fulfillment. Yet, I say to you—and beg you to believe me—multiply these tiny triumphs by a million, add them all together, and they are nothing—less than nothing, a positive impediment—measured against one draught of that living water Christ

offers to the spiritually thirsty, irrespective of who or what they are.

Unfortunately, there are thousands of people throughout our nation, in high schools, colleges, and the business world, who are convinced that wealth and success will bring meaning, contentment, and joy to their lives. But such is not the case. My experiences at ZZZZ Best and in prison have shown me, time and again, that wealth-driven appetites are insatiable. I have seen too many lives ruined by the pursuit of power and money.

For those of us who have learned these lessons the hard way, there is still hope. The message of Christ promises forgiveness and a future, the former best defined by a close friend at Lompoc when he said, "Forgiveness is giving up hope for a better yesterday"; the latter best expressed through the apostle Paul's exhortation that we give much energy to "forgetting the past and looking forward to what lies ahead" (Phil. 3:13 TLB).

The ZZZZ Best crime was a deliberate, ruthless sequence of events that harmed thousands of people. I have never lost sight of that. I never will. But if I can use my experiences at ZZZZ Best to convince people that the pursuit of worldly wealth at the expense of integrity is a one-way road leading nowhere, then and only then will I have accomplished something.